Classical Mythology: A Very Short Introduction

VERY SHORT INTRODUCTIONS are for anyone wanting a stimulating and accessible way in to a new subject. They are written by experts, and have been published in more than 25 languages worldwide.

The series began in 1995, and now represents a wide variety of topics in history, philosophy, religion, science, and the humanities. The VSI Library now contains over 200 volumes—a Very Short Introduction to everything from ancient Egypt and Indian philosophy to conceptual art and cosmology—and will continue to grow to a library of around 300 titles.

Very Short Introductions available now:

ADVERTISING Winston Fletcher
AFRICAN HISTORY John Parker and
   Richard Rathbone
AGNOSTICISM Robin Le Poidevin
AMERICAN POLITICAL PARTIES AND
   ELECTIONS L. Sandy Maisel
THE AMERICAN PRESIDENCY
   Charles O. Jones
ANARCHISM Colin Ward
ANCIENT EGYPT Ian Shaw
ANCIENT PHILOSOPHY Julia Annas
ANCIENT WARFARE Harry Sidebottom
ANGLICANISM Mark Chapman
THE ANGLO-SAXON AGE John Blair
ANIMAL RIGHTS David DeGrazia
ANTISEMITISM Steven Beller
THE APOCRYPHAL GOSPELS
   Paul Foster
ARCHAEOLOGY Paul Bahn
ARCHITECTURE Andrew Ballantyne
ARISTOCRACY William Doyle
ARISTOTLE Jonathan Barnes
ART HISTORY Dana Arnold
ART THEORY Cynthia Freeland
ATHEISM Julian Baggini
AUGUSTINE Henry Chadwick
AUTISM Uta Frith
BARTHES Jonathan Culler
BESTSELLERS John Sutherland
THE BIBLE John Riches
BIBLICAL ARCHEOLOGY Eric H. Cline
BIOGRAPHY Hermione Lee
THE BLUES Elijah Wald
THE BOOK OF MORMON Terryl Givens
THE BRAIN Michael O'Shea

BRITISH POLITICS Anthony Wright
BUDDHA Michael Carrithers
BUDDHISM Damien Keown
BUDDHIST ETHICS Damien Keown
CAPITALISM James Fulcher
CATHOLICISM Gerald O'Collins
THE CELTS Barry Cunliffe
CHAOS Leonard Smith
CHOICE THEORY Michael Allingham
CHRISTIAN ART Beth Williamson
CHRISTIAN ETHICS D. Stephen Long
CHRISTIANITY Linda Woodhead
CITIZENSHIP Richard Bellamy
CLASSICAL MYTHOLOGY Helen Morales
CLASSICS Mary Beard and John Henderson
CLAUSEWITZ Michael Howard
THE COLD WAR Robert McMahon
COMMUNISM Leslie Holmes
CONSCIOUSNESS Susan Blackmore
CONTEMPORARY ART Julian Stallabrass
CONTINENTAL PHILOSOPHY
   Simon Critchley
COSMOLOGY Peter Coles
THE CRUSADES Christopher Tyerman
CRYPTOGRAPHY Fred Piper and
   Sean Murphy
DADA AND SURREALISM David Hopkins
DARWIN Jonathan Howard
THE DEAD SEA SCROLLS Timothy Lim
DEMOCRACY Bernard Crick
DESCARTES Tom Sorell
DESERTS Nick Middleton
DESIGN John Heskett
DINOSAURS David Norman
DIPLOMACY Joseph M. Siracusa

For more information visit our web site:
www.oup.co.uk/general/vsi/

Helen Morales

CLASSICAL MYTHOLOGY

A Very Short Introduction

OXFORD
UNIVERSITY PRESS

OXFORD
UNIVERSITY PRESS

Great Clarendon Street, Oxford OX2 6DP

Oxford University Press is a department of the University of Oxford.
It furthers the University's objective of excellence in research, scholarship,
and education by publishing worldwide in

Oxford New York

Auckland Cape Town Dar es Salaam Hong Kong Karachi
Kuala Lumpur Madrid Melbourne Mexico City Nairobi
New Delhi Shanghai Taipei Toronto

With offices in

Argentina Austria Brazil Chile Czech Republic France Greece
Guatemala Hungary Italy Japan Poland Portugal Singapore
South Korea Switzerland Thailand Turkey Ukraine Vietnam

Oxford is a registered trade mark of Oxford University Press
in the UK and in certain other countries

Published in the United States
by Oxford University Press Inc., New York

British Library Cataloguing in Publication Data

Data available

Library of Congress Cataloging in Publication Data

Data available

ISBN 978–0–19–280476–1

9 10 8

Typeset by SPI Publisher Services, Pondicherry, India
Printed in Great Britain by
Ashford Colour Press Ltd, Gosport, Hampshire

Contents

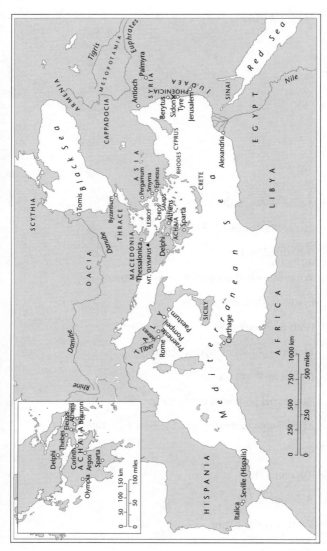

Map of ancient Greece, Italy, and other places discussed in this VSI

Acknowledgements

Thanks to the Faculty of Classics at the University of Cambridge, and to Newnham College for intellectual and financial support; to Richard Fletcher for research assistance; to Elizabeth Watson, Miriam Leonard, Emily Kneebone, and Benedict Wilkinson for reading and improving parts of the manuscript; to Emmanuelle Peri, Deborah Protheroe, James Thompson, and Luciana O'Flaherty at OUP; to Alyson Silverwood for copy-editing; to Augusta McMahon for assistance with the ancient Arabic material; to Margaret Malamud for help with the modern Arabic material; to Kristina Milnor for discussion of the Rockefeller Center; to Joseph Schwartz for guidance on psychoanalysis; to Simon Goldhill and Christopher Kelly and, for criticism and support from the beginning to the end, to Mary Beard and to Tony Boyle.

List of illustrations

1. Advertisement by the Greek National Tourism Organization. This advert, and others like it with the same caption, *Live Your Myth in Greece*, was widely seen in magazines and on buses in 2005

Introduction

In 2005 the Greek Ministry for Tourism published an advertisement that urged: LIVE YOUR MYTH IN GREECE.

The text at the top of the advert provides a gloss:

> Greece: a land of mythical dimensions. Where the spirit of hospitality welcomes you as a modern god. And the siren song draws you into its deep blue waters. Where a gentle breeze through ancient ruins seems to whisper your name. And a dance until dawn can take on Dionysian proportions. In Greece, the myths are still very much alive. And in amongst them sits your own ... patiently waiting for you to live it. Live your myth in Greece. Ask your travel agent.

We might think that the advert has scant respect for mythological tradition. To be drawn down into deep blue waters by a siren song was to meet with certain death (which is why the hero Odysseus plugged up the ears of his crew and tied himself to the ship's mast before sailing by the seductive singers). And a dance that takes on Dionysian proportions is probably best avoided (as Pentheus, the tragic king of Thebes, discovered when he was ripped limb from limb by his mother, one of Dionysus' dancing worshippers). But to respond to the advert with academic pedantry is to miss the point. What it is selling is a particular image of Greece – and of myth – one of prestige and pleasure, mystique and fantasy.

'Myth' functions in the advert in three different, but related, ways. The blurb and mermaid-like creature allude to myth as lore: the stories, the nuts and bolts of who did what to whom. The myth of Dionysus tells how he invented wine and incited women to ecstasy, for example. But there is another version of myth at work here: myth as ideological projection. It is a *myth* of modern Greece (whether true or not) that its past confers prestige upon its present. It is a story that Greece tells itself about itself repeatedly, in different contexts, and to different audiences. It is a myth that was projected in the entertainments that Greece put on when it was host nation both of the Eurovision Song Contest in 2006 and of the Olympic Games in 2004. When the advert urges us to 'live your myth', yet a further meaning of the word 'myth' is being used. This is myth as escapism, as thrill. LIVE YOUR MYTH means LIVE YOUR FANTASY.

This *Very Short Introduction* is concerned with all of these dimensions that together add up to what we call 'myth': lore, ideology, and pleasure. Scholars have produced as many definitions of myth as there are myths themselves. This book will discuss various definitions of myth as it goes along, but it is interested in myth as a *process* as much as a *thing*. I shall argue that the best way to answer the question of what classical mythology *is* is to look at what classical mythology *does*. What this book isn't is a series of potted retellings of myths, partly because this is a *very* short introduction, partly because there are many books that do that already (what one critic has called 'the paraphrase industry'), and partly because the aim of this book is to understand classical myths not as fossilized entities, but as living agents.

If 'myth' is a slippery term, so is 'classical'. It is common shorthand for 'ancient Greek and Roman'. But this shorthand has a history, and a bias. Since the Romantic movement, ancient Greece, renowned for its democracy, theatre, and philosophy, has come to stand for creativity and imagination, whereas Rome is known for its military and practical successes ('better sanitation and medicine and education, and irrigation and public health and roads and a freshwater system and baths and public order', as Reg puts it in *Monty Python's Life of Brian*). This book will look at the long dismissal of the Roman in 'classical' mythology, and ask whether 'mythology' wouldn't be equally as good an answer to the question, 'What have the Romans ever done for us?'

'Classical', like 'Classics', is also a value-laden term – think of the connotations of 'classical music', 'classic beauty', 'classic cars'. The myths of different cultures have been given different valences by their reception in so-called Western (and non-Western) culture. Those of ancient Greece and Rome have become *the* myths of the Western world. The label 'classical' acknowledges (and reinforces) their cultural supremacy over the myths of, say, ancient Egypt, Mesopotamia, and India. At the same time, it masks the Eurocentrism of this tradition. There's a smugness about the word and its pretensions to timeless and effortless superiority. An investigation of 'classical' myth is necessarily an investigation of cultural authority and its strategies and traditions.

Can we 'live our myths'? Well, no. Or very few of us, at least in the sense implied by the advert. Most of us don't play out our lives on such a grand and exaggerated scale as the heroes and heroines of classical myth (and we'd probably be locked up if we did). In any case, stories, events, and people require *collective* recognition to become *mythic*. If, while holidaying in Sparta, I have an affair with a gorgeous aristocrat and elope with him to Troy, that is my look-out and, at a pinch, a news story, but it is not a myth. Myths are stories that are of psychological importance to a community. My holiday romance, no matter how glamorous, is unlikely to fit the bill.

However, in another sense, we are all living classical myths, right here, right now. Classical mythology has been so influential upon Western culture that everyone who is alive to the art, culture, politics, and languages of today encounters it. This book is concerned both with showing how myths worked in their ancient contexts – in songs and shows, philosophy, art and argument – and with exploring classical myths from our most immediate points of engagement with them – from the politics, films, music, images, ideas, and beliefs that they still shape today. As this necessarily involves some sharp moves across different historical periods, the timeline at the back of the book is intended to help you orientate yourself.

This book aims to capture, and explore, the outrageousness, inventiveness, and sheer fun that characterize classical mythology. But it is also born of the conviction that myth *matters*. It mattered for the ancient Greeks and Romans, and it matters for us in understanding who we are: our selves, our liberties, and our lies.

Chapter 1

Without bulls there would be no Europe

Cultural currency

We meet classical myths in as ordinary ways as jangling loose change in our pockets. Every citizen and tourist of modern Greece must see the Greek 2 Euro coin (Figure 2) frequently, but I wonder how often anyone really looks at it. It displays the familiar image of a young woman, barely clothed, astride a swimming bull. The designers of the Euro, we are told, modelled their version on a mosaic in Sparta from the 3rd century AD, but Europa on the bull has become iconic, with versions painted by artists worldwide. It

Change ... and continuity. 2. A Greek 2 Euro coin from 2002, and 3. A Roman coin from Sidon from the 3rd century AD; both depicting Europa on the bull

depicts the myth usually referred to as 'the rape of Europa'. This account of the myth written by an anonymous ancient Greek scholar of uncertain date is less lurid than many:

> Zeus saw Europa the daughter of Phoenix, when she was gathering flowers in a meadow along with some nymphs, and he desired her. He came down and changed himself into a bull and breathed saffron breath from his mouth. In this way he deceived Europa, carried her off, took her to Crete, and had sex with her.

Isn't this a strange episode to depict on a coin? It's worth reflecting on what a picture of a mythical kidnapping is doing on our currency.

Images on coins are not randomly chosen. They function as emblems of the country that mints them. The Greek word 'Europe' means both the girl's name Europa, and the geographical and political entity, Europe. The double meaning isn't coincidental. As we shall see, the fortunes of the mythical figure and the region have been intimately connected from antiquity, though the precise nature of their relationship was complex and contested. The coin plays on the pun. It uses Europa to symbolize modern Europe. In doing so, it makes a powerful statement about national (and international) identities and cultural origins. The Euro was introduced in 2002 to mark a new world order: the creation of a new Europe, the European Union. At this moment of change the coin provides the reassurance of continuity; new Europe is also old Europe, with a long and venerable tradition that goes back to ancient Greece. The symbolism of Europa as Europe is a possessive one. It lays claim to ancient Greece as the ancestor of modern Europe. In so doing, it gives Europe, and modern Greece within it, roots in, and the pedigree of, classical antiquity.

The use of the Europa image is a significant part of Europe's reinvention of itself as the European Union. The symbol of 'Europe as Europa' has been paraded at particularly charged

4. Poster exhorting citizens to *Go and Vote* in the European elections in 1994

moments in Europe's history, times when the continent has been reconfigured and undergone radical change. The repetition of the symbol is strong in the material promoting the European Union. In the European Parliament Building in Brussels, Europa on the bull takes pride of place on a vast ceramic mural by Aligi Sassu that decorates the so-called Salon of Honour and is entitled *I miti del Mediterraneo* (The Myths of the Mediterranean). For the elections in 1994, the European Parliament's Office in Germany urged citizens *Wahlen Gehen* (Go and Vote) (Figure 4) through the charms of a game-show-hostess-cum-cheerleader Europa perched perkily atop her bull as he charges through the twelve stars of the Union.

The Europa myth was also used to sell the idea of European unification to children. A German children's book, *Die Euro Kids*, written in 1998 by Rolf Schonlau and Gabriele Knor, depicts Mario from Portugal, Astrid from Denmark, and their pals going on a tour of Europe and exploring the different countries and their currencies. They are followed around by a shady character wearing dark glasses and a yellow overcoat, who is later revealed to be the European Union Finance Minister. The Euro Kids visit Crete, where they tell a sanitized version of the rape of Europa. Alongside an illustration of the girl on a bull we are told, cryptically, 'Without bulls there would be no Europe.' When they return to Brussels, the Euro Kids give the President of the Union a souvenir: a hat made from two bull's horns stuck onto an old bathing cap.

A more sophisticated narrative (with no bull in sight) is to be found in the comic-strip adventures of Captain Euro and his sidekick Europa, a sexy blonde archaeologist who 'defends the security of Europe and upholds the values of the union'. Europa has impeccable (if confused) classicist credentials: she is an expert in ancient languages, investigates the myth of Atlantis, and gains her superpowers from an ancient tablet discovered while excavating Agamemnon's tomb. Together the superheroes save the world from Dr D. Vider and his posse of circus freaks. Captain Euro and Europa are the invention of *Twelve Stars Communications Ltd*, a PR agency hired by the European Commission to promote European unification.

The myth of Europa, then, in high art and popular culture, through private reading and public display, plays a formative role in the reinvention of modern Europe. Looking at some examples of this exposes the adaptability of myth. The myth of the rape of Europa is read very selectively in these modern representations. Her sexual encounter with Zeus is omitted (even as the image of her abduction is displayed repeatedly). If we are alert to the narrative of the myth, the question remains: isn't the rape of Europa a strange story to symbolize the European Union? What does it *mean*? Is the bull-god the President of the Union, snatching Europe away towards an unwanted economic and cultural union? (This is the interpretation innocently suggested by the Euro Kids' unfortunate gift.) Does it say: joining the EU means 'we're shafted'? Well, of course not. But editing out this interpretation is only possible if we read the myth as *emblem*, rather than *narrative*. Responding to myth often means wearing blinkers. Myth is a complex game of production and reception that involves selecting some parts of a narrative and suppressing others. As we shall see later on, this process of communication is not always easily controlled.

Turning Europa into an emblem of Europe makes this a myth of ancestry. Far from being a purely decorative motif, Europa on the bull is a politically freighted symbol. It is a good example of how classical myth can operate as a powerful ideological tool. It also shows how people of the modern world are not just analysers of ancient myth-making. In some respects we, no less than the ancients, actively use and exploit classical myth.

Myth was employed as an ideological tool in the ancient world too, in a remarkably similar way to the use of the Europa myth in modern Europe. Greek and Roman cities regularly claimed mythical ancestors for themselves. Heracles, Jason, and Perseus, heroes whose adventures involved them wandering around the world (and so could easily have led to them propagating ancestors far and wide), were most commonly posited. These claims to kinship were manipulated for diplomatic purposes. The historian Herodotus, writing in the 5th century BC, tells a story about an attempt by the Persian king, Xerxes, to persuade the people of Argos, a Greek city, not to fight with the other Greeks against the Persians. Xerxes' herald used the following appeal:

> Men of Argos, king Xerxes has this to say to you: 'According to our traditions, we are descended from Perses, whose father was Perseus, the son of Danaë, and Andromeda, the daughter of Cepheus. This means that we are descended from you Argives. And so it would be improper for us to make war against our ancestral line, and it would be improper for you to side with others who take up arms against us; instead, you should stay peacefully within your borders.'

This was winning rhetoric, at least until the Argives caved in under pressure from other Greeks. Almost two hundred years later, the Siboi, inhabitants of a city that found itself in the path of Alexander the Great and his troops, were more successful in using mythical kinship to their advantage. Both the Siboi and Alexander's people (the Macedonians) traced their origins back to the hero Heracles. Recognizing their common ancestry, Alexander spared the city.

In the Roman empire, Julius Caesar and Augustus exploited a tradition in which the Romans were said to have descended from the gods through the hero Aeneas, son of the goddess Venus. It is hard to know the extent to which the ancients understood their invented traditions to be fictive or historically accurate. Herodotus was sceptical about the Argive anecdote, and some cities went to extraordinarily convoluted lengths to argue for their relation to a particular hero, but claiming mythical kinship was a practice that persisted right into the early Christian era.

The very first reference to Europe as an area clearly distinguishable from the Peloponnesian islands and peninsula is found in the *Homeric Hymn to Apollo*, a song composed in the late 7th or early 6th century BC. At the time when Herodotus was writing, a century or so later, both the idea and the geography of Europe were rather vague. In fact, Herodotus was among the first Greeks to sketch out some boundaries for the continent, placing its western limit at the Adriatic, and its eastern near the Black Sea at the River Phasis (now Ruini in Georgia) or the River Tanais (now Don in Georgia). He is less clear about its northern and southern limits. Herodotus considers, but explicitly rejects, the idea that Europe was named after Europa:

> As for Europe… the origin of its name is uncertain, as is the identity of whoever first named the region – unless we say that Europa, the Tyrian princess, gave it her name, and that before her time it was just as nameless as the other continents. But it is plain that this Europa came from Asia and never set foot in what the Greeks now call Europe: she merely travelled from Phoenicia to Crete.

This is a good example of the complexity of the tradition. Already in the 5th century BC, when the idea that Europe was named after Europa was first being aired, we find a major Greek historian expressing scepticism about the idea.

It was Phoenicia, a civilization whose heartland was in the coastal plains of what is now modern Lebanon, that was the land most commonly associated by Greek writers with Europa, not Europe. Most took her to be the daughter of the Phoenician king Agenor, and sister of Cadmus and Phoenix, although others, including Homer and the unnamed scholar quoted at the beginning of this chapter, said she was the daughter of Phoenix (the ambiguity of the Greek word 'Phoinix' as meaning both the name 'Phoenix' and the term 'Phoenician' further complicates the picture). Coins were minted which depicted Europa on the bull above the name of a Phoenician city, in the case of the one in Figure 3, the important trading post of Sidon. This particular coin was produced between AD 218 and 222, after Rome, under the emperor Elagabalus, took over the city of Sidon. (The letters 'A' and 'P' on either side of the figures, and the inscription 'SIDON COL MET' underneath them, are short for 'Colonia Aurelia Pia Metropolis Sidon', which means 'The Metropolis of Sidon, a Roman outpost in honour of Marcus Aurelius'.) It shows that the association between Europa and Phoenicia continued, even and at the same time as Europa was also emerging as a symbol, more broadly, of Europe.

Looking from the ancient coin to the modern one, it is hard not to be struck by the similarity of the iconography. The way Europa is balancing on the bull with her right leg stretched forward, the way her robe has slipped down onto her legs revealing the rest of her body, the positioning of the bull as he swims off to the right of the image, leaping as he does so over the writing beneath, the framing of the image with a circle of stars or dots: all these have changed remarkably little in two millennia. Nor has the function of the image changed: it is still used, as it was then, to symbolize a region. Yet in one striking way, the mythical emblem has travelled far – at least as far as the girl in the story – from Phoenicia to Greece, and from the ancient world to the modern one.

The first writer to establish a connection between the myth of Europa and the continent was the poet Moschus. His poem *Europa*, written in Greek in the 2nd century BC, is an eroticized description of Zeus' deceit of Europa and their flight to Crete in which the princess is a naïve but willing captive. The night before the abduction, Europa dreams of 'two lands fighting to possess her: Asia, and the other land opposite' (not named). The lands are personified as women. Asia resembles 'a woman from her own country' and the other land, 'a stranger' who 'violently' seized

Europa 'with her powerful hands'. 'Who was this foreign land that I saw in my sleep?' cried the girl, upon wakening. 'How longing gripped my heart for her, and how desirously in turn did she take me into her arms like her child. I only pray to the blessed fates that the dream turn out well.'

It is in the Roman Empire, with Rome as leader of Europe, that the genealogy is made explicit. Making Europa the mythical ancestor of Europe is, in fact, more a Roman myth than a Greek one. In the 1st century BC, the poet Horace wrote an account of the myth in the third book of his collection of poems, the *Odes*. In it, the poet imagines the goddess Venus comforting Europa, who is enraged and suicidal after her seduction (as it is described here) by the bull:

> You do not know that you are the wife of almighty Jupiter. Stop
> your sobbing. Learn to endure your great good fortune: half of the
> world will bear your name.

Augustan Rome was a time of energetic European propaganda. And the image of Europa on the bull was a popular theme in art. Augustus, before he became emperor, was said to have plundered a famous Alexandrian fresco by the artist Antiphilus (now lost) while fighting in Egypt. The fresco depicted Europa and her brother Cadmus, who went looking for her after she had been abducted. According to the satirist Martial, paintings of Europa adorned the Temple of the Divine Augustus and a portico was named after Europa in a public area of the city. All of this in the service of Roman propaganda promoting Europe, in the words of the writer Pliny, as 'by far the finest of all lands'.

The myth (lore) of Europa may have remained largely the same from archaic Greece to Augustan Rome, and the iconography of her riding the bull showed remarkable constancy, but the myth (ideology) of Europa changed at different periods for different political and cultural ends. The example of Europa alone shows how some of the models currently used for thinking about classical mythology are inadequate. It is often said nowadays that Roman myths are pale imitations of Greek myths, or that the Romans had no mythology of their own, positions that drastically misrepresent how myths worked. Likewise, classical myth is often talked about as if it were a homogeneous and static category. Instead, as we have seen, the ideological impact of myths changed *within* the ancient world. This is necessarily so, for myth operated – and operates – as cultural currency.

Kernels of truth

In the United States of America since 1987, the Europa myth has meant something very different. 1987 saw the publication of *Black Athena: The Afroasiatic Roots of Classical Civilisation*, the first instalment of a multi-volume project by Martin Bernal, a British scholar now lecturing in the US. To say that *Black Athena* has been controversial would be an understatement. 'The most discussed book on the ancient history of the eastern Mediterranean world since the Bible' hypes one scholar. It is a reasonable gloss on the reaction, in academic circles and beyond, excited by Bernal's work. *Black Athena* sought to challenge the prevalent view that Western civilization has its roots in ancient Greece. It argues that from as early as the 18th century BC, the ancient Egyptians and Phoenicians (which together Bernal terms 'Afroasiatic') exerted immense cultural influence upon the Greeks. He writes:

> I argue that there is a need for a radical reassessment of the image of Ancient Greece and that we should turn from one of a civilisation which sprang – like Athena from the head of Zeus – virgin and fully formed, to one in which Greece grew up at the intersection of Europe, Africa, and Asia as a thoroughly mixed and eclectic culture. The greatness and extraordinary brilliance of Greek civilisation in antiquity was not the result of isolation and cultural purity but of

frequent contact with and stimulus from the many surrounding peoples on the already heterogeneous natives of the Aegean.

The ancient Greeks themselves acknowledged these debts, argues Bernal, and even ties of kinship with the Egyptians and Phoenicians. Their view of cultural origins he terms the 'Ancient model'. It is from the 19th century onwards that scholars, unable to accept that Western civilization originated with Africans and Jews (equated by Bernal, controversially, with ancient Egyptians and Phoenicians respectively), have dismissed or denied their influences on ancient Greece. Their model of cultural purity Bernal calls the 'Aryan model'. In other words, because of scholars' prejudices, we've got the ancient world, and the West, all wrong. This is a powerful accusation (and one that had been made before by some Afrocentrist scholars, whose work paved the way for Bernal's thesis). So powerful that it has had the salutary effect of making many classicists take a step back and re-examine their assumptions.

Bernal's argument rests on a wide variety of material: literary, archaeological, and linguistic. But central to his thesis – and to his critics' rejection of it – is the question of *how to read classical myth*. The Europa myth is of particular importance to him, but he is less interested in Europa's abduction than in what happened afterwards. In various accounts, when Agenor, Europa's father and king of the Phoenician city of Tyre, heard about his daughter's abduction, he sent her brothers, Cadmus and Phoenix, in pursuit of her. The brothers were unsuccessful and became distracted from their mission, ultimately settling down and founding cities on the Greek mainland. Most famously, Cadmus was said to have founded Thebes.

Bernal reads this myth as evidence for an early Phoenician invasion and colonization of the Greek mainland. He contends that this and other myths of origin contain 'a kernel of truth'.

He reads them as preserving 'historical elements', though he admits the impossibility of extracting these with any precision. Reading myth as crystallizing historical fact was a common approach in the 19th and early 20th centuries. But it is an approach to myth that is fraught with problems. It ignores or takes insufficient account of how mythic narratives are exploited for political purposes. As we have already seen, those who lived in antiquity invented, and reinvented, their traditions no less than we do now. Rather than reading the myth of Cadmus' founding of Thebes as (in some sense) documentary evidence for real, historical colonization, it might be more profitable to look at who was telling the myth and why. The majority of the accounts of the myth are found in Athenian sources. Athens had a long history of rivalry with Thebes. The Athenians were keen to establish the origins of other Greek cities in marked contrast to their own. The story they told of Athenian origins was one of autochthony, which means they were born from the earth. Athenians were very proud of being indigenous to their land. Myths that dramatize the contrast between their indigenous origins and other cities' foundation by external settlers rehearse this pride. This *Greek* myth is an avowedly *Athenian* myth and reflects Athenian political interests. It is a problem for us that much of our evidence reflects this bias. Does all this mean that Bernal's thesis is simply wrong? I don't think it does. Ultimately, the origins of Greek culture remain impossible to identify with any confidence. What is clear is the difficulty of reading myths as containing 'kernels of truth'.

However, the modern reinvention of Europa as a European myth – and not just in its nastier manifestations of Captain Euro, Europa, and their stereotyped enemies – seems to me to be a popular culture version of what Bernal identified as post-18th-century scholarship's 'Aryan model' of cultural origins. New Europe is designed as having its origins in ancient Greece, and the Europa myth is stamped as a European myth. But classical myth isn't a European possession, or even a Western one. Its dialogue with the modern world is far more widespread. A history of the full extent of classical mythology's impact upon non-Western cultures has yet to be written. I'm going to end this chapter with just one example.

Classical myths, especially Greek myths, have consciously and deliberately been used by modern Arabic poets, most notably the important avant-garde poets Nazik al Mala'ika, 'Abd al-Wahhab al-Bayati, and Badr Shakir al-Sayyab, who were influential in the 1950s. The title of al-Bayati's poem 'Greetings, Athens' wryly announces its dialogue with the past. In the poem, the Greek gods are cruel and the world needs a poet, a Ulysses, to break free from his chains and liberate it:

> The sun is in a detention camp
> Guarded by dogs and hills
> Perhaps a thousand nights have passed
> And still
> Penelope waits
> Weaving the garment of fire,
> Or Ulysses still in chains
> On the island of the impossible
> Perhaps on Mount Olympus
> Greek gods are still begging
> The barren lightning on the mountains
> Their food is wine and bread
> And the suffering of millions of men.
> I said: 'Greetings'
> And my heart wept
> And in the ruins, the dawn
> Lit the new face of the world,
> The face of a poet breaking his chains.

These poets were influenced by the so-called 'Apollo group', writers who gathered in the 1930s and were regular contributors to a literary journal called *Abullu* (Apollo). *Abullu* was founded by Ahmad Zaki Abu Shadi, a poet and a doctor who studied in England before returning to Egypt in 1932. The journal itself was short-lived, but its impact was not. Its purpose, emphasized in articles and editorials, was to acknowledge that Arabic literature was inspired by the mythology of ancient Greece and claimed a share in its legacy. This mission statement was probably more important politically than it was for the poetry published by the journal. As one contributor commented, the idea was that 'Arabic culture should be seen at least in part as "the fruit of the Greek mind"'. These Arabic poets staked their claim to ancient mythology and the cultural authority it bears no less fiercely than their modern European counterparts.

Who we are, where we came from, and what we want to be: there's a lot at stake in a myth.

Chapter 2
Contexts, then and now

Being educated

After their adventures in Crete, the Euro Kids stop off in Italy, where they spend their Euros on a visit to the Archaeological Museum in Naples. There they see an original Roman painting of Europa. The painting (Figure 5) is a fresco from the so-called 'House of Jason' in the Italian city of Pompeii, and dates to some time between 15 BC and AD 15. Pompeii is one of our richest resources for artistic representations of classical mythology. Many of its masterpieces are now housed in the Naples museum, safe from future volcanic eruptions, the weather, and tourists. The museum is a veritable warehouse of myth. But each artwork has been removed from its original context, and without our being aware of where and how it would originally have been seen, much of what that particular representation of myth would have meant for its Roman viewers is lost.

This Europa was originally seen in a bedroom in a Pompeian house. The bedroom had three separate mythological frescoes on three different walls. Next to Europa was a painting of Pan, the god who was half-man, half-goat, with his lovers, the nymphs. Opposite Pan was a painting of the hero Hercules shown at his moment of victory over the centaur Nessus. Both Nessus and Hercules are rivals for the love of Deianeira. Hercules is the

5. Roman wall painting of Europa from a house in Pompeii

victor, and the painting depicts Nessus dying, having been shot by Hercules' arrow. Deianeira is standing behind him covering her face. (Nessus' revenge comes later on in the narrative, when the 'love potion' he gives to Deianeira on his deathbed turns out to be deadly poison and leads Deianeira, unwittingly, to kill Hercules.)

The Europa painting was not viewed in isolation, then, but as part of a design. The spatial arrangement encourages the viewer to make links between the three images. Perhaps a common theme of the violence of desire is implied, as Europa is about to be snatched away, Pan is known for raping nymphs, and the centaur has just assaulted Deianeira as he carried her across the river. The painting of Europa has a different resonance in this context than if it had been placed in a series of paintings of Zeus' abductions, say, or of other myths of Cretan girls. Examining how the images in this room relate to others in the rest of the house would further expand connections between the pictures. The house makes you work hard at reading the myths and how they interrelate. Looking at images of myths in museums can make them seem like mere decorations. They were decorative, but what they meant to their original viewers was determined by how they were positioned *in relation* to other images and other myths.

Being able to play the game, to join in the discussions that took place around these paintings, was the mark of an educated man. It was important for a Roman of this period to get his Greek mythology *right*. Being able to identify who was who and what was what was a sign that the viewer was a person of culture and status. Latin literature gives us some wonderful caricatures of those who don't know their myth. In Petronius' novel *Satyrica*, Trimalchio, the grotesque host of a lavish banquet, is exposed as being a social climber (an ex-slave and *nouveau riche*) when he gets his mythology ludicrously muddled.

Greek mythology was, therefore, an essential part of an elite Roman's education. He would learn the myths from a core curriculum of literary works, as well as from art and religious ritual. The epics of Homer, the *Iliad* and the *Odyssey*, were key texts. They had long been treated as morally and culturally authoritative. As early as the 6th century BC, when the poems were sung as part of the Panathenaea, the great civic festival in Athens in honour of its patron goddess Athena, the *Iliad* and *Odyssey* had become canonical. Hesiod's poems *Theogony* (on the Greek gods) and *Works and Days* (on how to live a good life) were also part of the curriculum, as were the tragedies of Aeschylus, Sophocles, and, most especially, Euripides. The comedies of Menander and poetry of Pindar were also popular.

There was no single work – no lengthy epic or compendium – that told all the myths, from start to finish. And yet there was so much myth. In a time when social embarrassment was a forgotten nymph's name away, a busy Roman with pretensions to culture had his work cut out being able to identify all the mythological allusions he came across in literature, oratory, and art. That's where mythography came in. Mythographers wrote handbooks of myth that retold the stories from Homer, Hesiod, Euripides, and other classics in as clear a way as possible. The term 'mythography' first appears in Strabo, writing in the 1st century AD, but mythography had been popular since around 300 BC. Rarely interested in aesthetic or other interpretations of the myths, mythographies were essentially crib sheets: A to Zs of myth. Because it is not 'proper literature', modern scholars have tended to overlook mythography. But much of the mythological lore whose knowledge we take for granted comes from works such as Apollodorus' *Library of Mythology*, Antonius Liberalis' *Metamorphoses*, or the works of Ptolemy Chennus (Ptolemy 'the Quail'), all written in the first two centuries AD, rather than from Homer or Euripides.

This attitude to Greek mythology in the Roman empire created an atmosphere of *mythological correctness*; erudition for erudition's sake. Schoolchildren learned the details of mythological narratives in the dullest way imaginable. This exercise on the Trojan War is from Egyptian schools and is repeated in seven papyri from the 2nd to the 6th centuries AD, an indication of how commonly it must have been used:

'Which gods helped the Hellenes?' Hera, Athena, Hermes, Poseidon, Hephaestus. 'Which gods helped the barbarians?' Ares, Aphrodite, Apollo, Artemis, Leto, Scamander. 'Who was the king of the Trojans?' Priam. 'Who was their general?' Hector. 'Who were his counsellors?' Polydamas and Agenor. 'Who were their prophets?' Helenus and Cassandra, children of Priam. 'Who were their heralds?' Idaeus and Eumedes, Dolon's father; perhaps Dolon as well.

An anecdote makes fun of this scholastic pedantry: 'the ignorant grammarian, when stumped by the question: "Who was the mother of Priam?" replied, "Out of respect we call her Ma'am"'.

Mythological correctness was, in any case, a kind of fraud. The mythographers competed with each other for the most ingenious genealogies, citing, and sometimes *creating*, sources as authorities for their information. The way that classical myths are often told and read nowadays gives the impression that there is one 'main' version of a myth, and that myths are traditional tales, handed down over the centuries. This is both true and untrue. Tales of the Trojan War, for example, were told by Homer and epic poets, and revised and retold by playwrights, poets, vase painters, and novelists throughout Greek and Roman times and beyond. However, we shouldn't underestimate the role that mythographers, artists, and dramatists played as *innovators* of mythology. It is likely that Ptolemy the Quail fabricated much of the mythological lore in his mythographies. Certainly Euripides, perhaps the most radical of the classical Athenian playwrights, created new myths, or changed the old ones so drastically that it must have seemed to some to be a travesty. His tragedy *Medea* has given us the most popular account of the story in which Medea is betrayed by her hero husband Jason, and kills their children in revenge. But this was Euripides' invention; previous versions had Medea protect her children.

Modern tellers of ancient myths are no less creative than were the ancient mythographers and poets. Robert Graves's compilation *The Greek Myths*, written in 1955, is a classic work that still today is many people's first introduction to Greek mythology. (We'll return to Graves in Chapter 7.) Despite the impression of meticulous scholarship, some of *The Greek Myths* is very much Graves's own invention. And there are those who would say that it's all the better for it.

Wolfgang Peterson's 2004 film *Troy* failed to win the hearts of many modern audiences. This, despite the vogue for 'epic' film sparked by the success of Ridley Scott's *Gladiator* a few years earlier, and despite casting one of the most bankable superstars in Hollywood, Brad Pitt, as the hero Achilles (Figure 6). The critics were too 'mythologically correct'. They took exception to the deviation of the script from the story in Homer's *Iliad*. Briseis kills Agamemnon. Helen and Paris live happily ever after. Peterson had got his myth wrong. But the film might be seen in a more positive light as taking its place in a long and distinguished tradition of mythological innovation. Peterson understood the nature of myths better than his critics. *Troy* is an essentially Euripidean film.

Not everyone in the ancient world thought an education in mythology was for the good. In Terence's comic drama *Eunuch* (161 BC), a young man, bent on seduction, looks at a painting of Zeus seducing Danaë. Zeus transformed himself into a shower of golden rain and so was able (literally) to drop into the girl's lap. Emboldened by the god's example, the young man embarks upon his own ploys. St Augustine, in his *Confessions*, singles out this episode to demonstrate the evils of students learning from mythological models. (The Euro Kids, you might be reassured to learn, were bored when they looked at the painting of Europa.) Augustine's anxieties that mythology might encourage imitation of immoral exploits echoes those famously voiced centuries earlier by Socrates in Plato's *Republic*. In this

6. **Brad Pitt as Achilles in the film *Troy* (2004)**

dialogue, Plato imagines Socrates discussing what's best practice for an ideal state with Plato's elder brothers, Glaucon and Adeimantos.

> Our first business, it seems, is to supervise the storytellers and to choose their stories only when they are edifying and reject them

25

when they aren't. And we'll persuade nurses and mothers to tell our chosen stories to their children, since they will shape their children's souls with stories much more than they do their bodies by handling them. Many of the stories they tell now, however, must be thrown out.

When pressed for examples, Socrates suggests that Homer, Hesiod, and any other poets who compose 'false stories' are at fault. He is particularly upset by tales in which gods and heroes set a bad example:

> [Such stories] should not be told in our city, Adeimantos. Nor should any young person hear it said that in committing the most heinous crimes he's doing nothing out of the ordinary… he's only doing the same as the first and greatest of the gods.

Out goes Hesiod's account of how Saturn, Zeus' father, devoured his children, and how Zeus punished him for it and seized power. Out goes Homer's tale of the battle of the gods in the *Iliad*. Out goes anything that depicts a god or hero behaving badly. Most myth, then, must go.

To most people now this has a sour tang of censorship about it, yet it is interesting to reflect upon how we present Greek mythology to children today. The bestselling children's books by William J. Bennett, American author and former Secretary of State of Education under Ronald Reagan, frequently include tales from Greek myth. They are strongly sanitized and come with a clear moral message. In *The Book of Virtues: A Treasury of Great Moral Stories*, he tells an account of Icarus who, together with his craftsman father Daedalus, was said to have fled from the captivity of King Minos of Crete by flying through the air on wings made from feathers and wax. Daedalus escaped safely, but Icarus flew too close to the sun. The wax melted and he fell to the sea and drowned. Bennett uses the myth to inculcate good behaviour:

This famous Greek myth reminds us exactly why young people have a responsibility to obey their parents – for the same good reason parents have a responsibility to guide their children: there are many things adults know that young people do not… Safe childhoods and successful upbringings require a measure of obedience, as Icarus finds out the hard way.

All this is very Platonic: the story doesn't illustrate, say, the indifference to mortals of the gods, or Daedalus' bravery in rebelling against a king, but a moral that will (according to Bennett) benefit the family and the state. Indeed, it is self-consciously in the Platonic tradition: the frontispiece to the book quotes Socrates' views on myth in Plato's *Republic*.

The National Curriculum of England, Wales, and Northern Ireland provides a rather different model. It says that children should be taught 'myths, legends, and traditional stories' at Key Stage 2 (for 9-, 10-, and 11-year-olds). The following is an extract of a lesson plan for a mythology project from a teacher's manual:

What to do during the lesson

Either remind children about the Greek myth they have recently read *or* do a shared reading of a Greek myth involving the gods.

Talk with the children about the Greek gods and their special roles. Together try to complete profiles for gods the children know about, using the following worksheet pattern:

Name of god/goddess_____
Has powers over_____
Positive characteristics_____
Negative characteristics_____
Symbol_____

Groups of children can be set the activity of completing this profile for all the gods and goddesses they have heard of, including:

27

Zeus, Hera, Poseidon, Hades, Athena, Aphrodite, Apollo, Hermes, Ares.

So far, so Ptolemy the Quail. The suggested follow-up activities, however, are rather different:

Create 2 nature myths 2–5 paragraphs long. Use worksheets with the following prompts for the children:

Choose an object or an event in nature (e.g. a rainbow, an earthquake, thunder)

Where does the object come from, or what causes the event?

What characters are involved in the myth?

Write a 2–5 paragraph myth about the object or the event in nature.

Tell the children that these myths should explain the object or the event. For example, they can explain how and why a specific animal was created and/or why there are earthquakes.

Create a mythological hero and a mythological creature. Write short stories about these characters.

The Key Stage 2 lesson plan credits adults with more discrimination in the teaching of mythology than Plato did. These children are invited to think about myths as reflecting or explaining events from nature (an approach to myth called 'euhemerism', to which we shall return later, in Chapter 4). Moreover, in the lesson plan the students are encouraged to create their own myths. Altogether a more imaginative formal education in Greek myth (if a considerably less thorough one) than that undertaken by a child in the early Roman empire.

Living myths

If the Romans (and Greeks) living in the Roman empire had a sense of 'Greek mythology' as a discrete body of material, it was because they had sufficient distance from the rituals and practices within which Greek myths first emerged. Whereas Greeks (and Romans) living a long time before the Roman empire, in the archaic and classical periods, would have been puzzled by the notion that they had a 'mythology' as such. For them, gods and heroes were part of everyday life. And not just in religious life. Also in politics, law, entertainment, philosophy, and science. Likewise, the inhabitants of the Roman empire were much less likely to be aware of 'Roman mythology' *as a mythology*, even as they were highly self-conscious manipulators of earlier Greek and Roman mythological narratives and symbols. When we are living with, through, and around myths, we are too close to them to recognize them as 'mythology'. Some distance is needed to see mythology as a separate body of knowledge.

Let's illustrate this by taking a tour of the Palatine Hill in Rome (Figure 7) as it was in the day of the poet Ovid (43 BC to AD 17). This was a highly fashionable neighbourhood, where the emperor Augustus lived. One of the seven hills of Rome, the Palatine was, according to myth, the place where Romulus and Remus, twin sons of Rhea Silvia (or, in some versions, Ilia) and the god Mars, were exposed to die but then rescued and suckled by a she-wolf. It is also the place where the adult Romulus was said to have

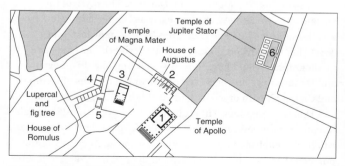

7. **The Palatine Hill in Augustan Rome**

founded the city of Rome. The Casa Romuli ('Hut of Romulus') on the southwest corner of the hill was said to be where Romulus had lived and was preserved as a memorial to Rome's founder. The Lupercal marked where Romulus and Remus were supposed to have been fed by the wolf with a sacred precinct that displayed bronze statues of the boys nursing and even the very fig tree under which a shepherd was said to have discovered them.

Nearby, and next to the emperor Augustus' house, was the Temple of Apollo, an impressive building of white Italian marble, and the most famous of the Roman shrines to Apollo. It was built in 28 BC, three years after the victory of Augustus over Anthony and Cleopatra at the Battle of Actium. Apollo is frequently represented in Latin poetry as having helped Augustus (then called Octavian) win the battle, and, in a brilliant and characteristic piece of Augustan propaganda, the temple and its god became associated with the emperor's triumph. In the *Aeneid*, Virgil's vivid account of Augustus' victory climaxes with the image of the emperor seated in the Temple of Apollo: an anachronistic image, but a powerful one.

A famous portico, known as the Portico of the Danaids, either surrounded or adjoined the temple. It displayed statues of Danaus and his 50 daughters, the Danaids. The myth of the Danaids was well known from as early as Homer's time. It was the subject of an epic poem, the *Danais* (now lost), and Aeschylus' tragedy *Suppliants* (which survives). The story, as a mythographer would have it, runs something like this: Aegyptus and Danaus were brothers (and, incidentally, cousins of Europa and Cadmus), both of whom had 50 children; Aegyptus sons, and Danaus daughters. They fought bitterly over who should rule Egypt, with the result that Danaus fled Egypt and settled in Argos, where he established himself as king. However, Aegyptus' enmity pursued them, as his 50 sons claimed their right, as kin, to marry their cousins. The denouement is as gloriously extravagant and horrifying as any in Greek myth. Danaus agrees to the match, but gives each girl a dagger with orders to kill her husband on their wedding night. All obeyed, except Hypermestra, who (perhaps for love) spared her husband Lynceus. Hypermestra and Lynceus became ancestors of future kings of Argos, including the hero Perseus. The other sisters were punished in the Underworld, condemned to pour water into a leaking receptacle, over and over, for ever and ever.

As always, the bare narrative, the lore, is only part of what makes a myth a myth. The ancient Greeks had a collective psychological and religious investment in this story. It became important for thinking about and practising the institution and rituals of marriage. Hypermestra became established as the first priestess of Hera, sovereign goddess of Argos, who had special dominion over marriage and domesticity. Her sisters' punishment in the Underworld was to perform, for eternity, an imitation of the *loutrophoria*, the essential ritual of marriage involving the pouring of pure water. The Danaids were also said to have introduced to Athens, from Egypt, the ritual of the Thesmophoria, a three-day-long festival attended only by wives, which, among other things, affirmed the institution of marriage. The myth's operation is rich, tense, paradoxical. Marriage is legitimated, yet founded in violence and bloodshed. The context of the Portico of the Danaids on the Palatine is quite different from that of a marriage ceremony in classical Greece. The myth is the same, but not the same. The most obvious interpretation of the Portico is that it monumentalizes Augustus' conquest of Cleopatra's Egypt. As the Danaids vanquished the sons of Aegyptus, so the Romans conquered the Egyptians. Yet this symbolism is paradoxical, too. The Danaids were impious, deserving of eternal punishment. Not a desirable association, one would think, for Augustus' Romans.

Moving on past the temples of Juno Sospita (Juno Saviour), Jupiter Stator (Jupiter the Stayer), and another (most probably) to Jupiter Invictus (Jupiter Invincible), we come to the temple of Magna Mater. Magna Mater, also known as Cybele, was the Great Mother goddess of Anatolia, whose cult involved ecstatic dancing and castration. Magna Mater was known in classical Greece, where she was associated with the goddess Demeter (both were concerned with agriculture and fertility), but it was not until 204 BC that her cult was officially introduced to Rome. The goddess was associated with Mount Ida, near Troy. This connection was important to the Romans because they traced their ancestry back to the Trojan hero Aeneas (and so to his mother, Venus, and to her father, Jupiter).

Romulus and Remus, whose origins are controversial but whose story becomes identified as a singularly Roman myth, rub shoulders with Apollo and the Danaids, figures appropriated from Greek narratives, and Magna Mater, an exotic import. Yet all these myths, functioning as part of a civic design to promote Augustan ideology, are very much *Roman* myths. The Palatine Hill instructs us how myths work. Less as 'mythology' in any unique sense, than as everyday life. The religious and political operations of myths are very much in evidence here, as well as their aesthetic appeal. It is a crucial insight that to understand classical myth we need to have some knowledge of what the scholar Marcel Detienne calls its 'ethnographic context'. That is, the particular cultural and religious practices at any one place and time which structure and give meaning to the bare bones of the narratives. Contrary to common assumption, myths are not timeless. Or, at least, the lore may be, but the meanings of a myth – its energy and impact – are very much dependent upon its contexts.

Leaping Louie and Goldenballs

This is as true for classical myth now as it was in antiquity, as I shall explore by looking at two golden Prometheuses from the last century. Many of the representations of classical mythology in architecture today attest above all else to the banality of public art.

On pediments, arches, and doorways, from public monuments to banks, motifs from classical myth are all too common. But nothing is banal in and of itself. Rather, such adornments are the result of a lengthy history of appropriating the classical and making it part of our visual repertoire. So much so that the individual impact of each image is easily lost. Take the Brandenburg Gate in Berlin. This imposing structure has a central gateway divided into five arches with pediments and a striking chariot with horses above. The dividing walls between the arches are decorated with 20 reliefs depicting the labours and exploits of Heracles. It's possible, of course, to interpret these images of heroism in relation to the others on the monument and with reference to the history of the Gate, but the height of the reliefs makes it unlikely they have much of an impact on most people. They give an impression of heroism and classicism, perhaps, but little more. The same cannot be said, however, of the architecture of the Rockefeller Center in New York city.

One of the most ambitious architectural projects of the last century, the Center, now a hub of media buildings and shops, is dominated by the Generic Electric (GE) building which towers over a sunken plaza. It is the creation of John D. Rockefeller Jr, the philanthropist son of the oil tycoon. Rockefeller wanted his architecture to *mean* something and employed many celebrated artists to help him realize this vision. The motif was intended to be that of 'New Frontiers', but the symbolism of the Rockefeller Center is so overdetermined, it is quite hard to discern any coherent design. Over the front entrance to the GE building is a huge god-like figure (in fact inspired by William Blake's Jehovah), who brandishes his compass over the inscription 'Wisdom and Knowledge shall be the Stability of our Times' (a quotation from the biblical Isaiah). On the Sixth Avenue entrance there's a mosaic mural with an opaque and overpopulated allegory ('Thought', 'Publicity', 'Cruelty', 'Hygiene'… and many more). With a giant statue of Atlas, relief of Mercury, and allegories of 'Gifts to Earth for Mankind' in the Center complex, and murals of 'Labor

8. Paul Manship's statue *Prometheus* (1934)

Collaborating with Art', 'American Progress', and 'Time' inside the GE building, the Rockefeller Center screams its significance without making clear what the significance is.

The jewel in Rockefeller's crown is a dazzling 18-foot-long, 8-ton statue of Prometheus (Figure 8). According to myth (notably told by the poet Hesiod in his *Theogony*, and the playwright Aeschylus in his *Prometheus Bound*), Prometheus stole fire from the gods (by hiding a flame in a fennel stalk) and brought it to earth to benefit mankind. The gift of fire brought civilization to mortals: they could cook food, do metalwork, and make medicines. Zeus, enraged at Prometheus' deception, had Kratos (Strength) and Bia (Force) bind him to a mountain in the Caucasus. There, an eagle swooped down and pecked out his liver each day. Prometheus, being a Titan (a divine figure whose race reigned supreme before Zeus and the Olympians took over), did not die. Instead, his liver grew back each night, and he remained in a state of unbearable torment until the hero Heracles came by and shot the eagle.

The work of celebrated sculptor Paul Manship, Rockefeller's golden Prometheus was erected at the end of the sunken plaza, in front of the GE building, in 1934. Behind it is an inscription with a quotation from Aeschylus' *Prometheus Bound*: 'Prometheus, teacher in every art, brought the fire to Earth that hath proven to mortals a means to mighty ends.' (Actually, a misquotation: in the play, it's fire, not Prometheus, that's the teacher.) Critics were snide. A cartoon by Robert Day in *The New Yorker* showed two women and a guard standing near the statue, with one of the women asking, 'Pardon me, but is that meant to be permanent?' People said Prometheus looked like he'd 'just sprung out of a bowl of hot soup' or like a 'young man escaping from his marriage ties'. He was nicknamed 'Leaping Louie'. I'm not convinced that Manship's *Prometheus* offended on aesthetic grounds alone. Rather, it went against received ideas about the use of classical myth. Its garish pop-culture glitter, coded as commercial and disposable in North American culture and a million miles away from the faded white marble of the Brandenburg Gate, unsettles the discourse of classical myth as indissociable from high culture.

It was also, it could have been argued, a strikingly *un-American* use of myth. The Founding Fathers of America harked back to classical exempla and imagery, but were uneasy about the associations of classical myth with aristocracy, especially heroes celebrated by the Roman empire, like Aeneas. The most famous of all American monuments, the Statue of Liberty, self-consciously and explicitly rejects classical models (although in doing so also acknowledges their importance). No quotation from Aeschylus on this icon's pedestal; rather, a poem by Emma Lazarus, entitled *The New Colossus*. The poem opens: 'Not like the brazen giant of

Greek fame,/ With conquering limbs astride from land to land;/ Here at our sea-washed, sunset gates shall stand/ A mighty woman with a torch, whose flame/ Is the imprisoned lightning, and her name/Mother of Exiles.' Lazarus imagines Liberty herself spurning classical myth: '"Keep ancient lands, your storied pomp!" cries she/ With silent lips.' The Rockefeller Center, in contrast, embraces 'storied pomp'. At the other end of the plaza, raised at a level so the visitor can read them and keep the Prometheus statue in their line of sight, are two plaques inscribed with John D. Rockefeller Jr's ten-point personal credo. It is a liberal and capitalist manifesto: 'I believe in the supreme worth of the individual and in his right to life, liberty and the pursuit of happiness', he proclaims. It alludes to the Prometheus narrative in a way that celebrates Prometheus as a challenger of state authority and as a self-sacrificing hero: 'I believe that the law was made for man and not man for the law; that government is the servant of the people and not their master', and 'I believe that the rendering of useful service is the common duty of mankind and that only in the purifying fire of sacrifice is the dross of selfishness consumed and the greatness of the human soul set free.'

'The dross of selfishness' is a good phrase to describe the targets of the feature film that stars our second golden Prometheus: commercialism, corporate greed, and the callous indifference of authoritarian regimes around the world. Tony Harrison's *Prometheus*, released in the UK in 1998, is a passionate lament for the devastation caused to the world by the misuse of technology. An ambivalent relationship is taken to Prometheus's gift of fire and the industrialization it has enabled. Harrison explicitly writes his screenplay through and against Aeschylus' *Prometheus Bound*. The Aeschylean characters are transposed to the bleak wastelands of Thatcher's England during the miners' strikes in the 1980s. Kratos and Bia become sinister workers in a nuclear power station. The characters speak in slick rhyming verse and quote from *Prometheus Bound* in Greek and English translation. If some of this description makes the film sound like an awkward

9. The statue of Prometheus in Tony Harrison's film, *Prometheus* (1998)

undergraduate production, well, it is (Harrison's budget was
pitifully small). But the power of the piece lies in its searing
evocation of the sheer scale of human suffering and the failure of
Promethean resistance to Zeus' despotism across the centuries
and the world:

> Whoever looks into the golden eyes of
> Prometheus set in the cremated
> sockets sees the early hope of the
> world and knows its late despair.

The spirit of Prometheus is embodied in a former Yorkshire coal
miner whose dialogues with Hermes, Zeus' cruel henchman, are
brilliant articulations of oppression and defiance. The image of
Prometheus is that of a colossal gold statue, made from the bodies
of melted-down miners, which is driven to places decimated by
fire, including Auschwitz, Dresden, and (Figure 9) the industrial
complex of Nowa Huta, in Poland. Hermes' desire is for the

inhabitants of these cities to turn on Prometheus and blame him for their suffering, rather than Zeus. Some do, but not the workers at Nowa Huta, much to the gods' fury:

> I should have known those stubborn Poles
> still had Prometheus in their souls.
> It angers Zeus. It riles. It galls
> Such grovelling to Goldenballs.

Prometheus has long been identified with the socialist struggle, and Harrison's hero pays homage to this tradition. In the introductory essay to his screenplay, Harrison acknowledges its relation to Percy Bysshe Shelley's *Prometheus Unbound*, a connection so intimately felt that Harrison first sketched ideas for the film in the Baths of Caracalla in Rome where, 180 years before, Shelley had written his play. Shelley's Prometheus, born of the failure of the French Revolution, was 'the saviour and the strength of the suffering man'. Since Shelley, Prometheus has been treated as, in one Marxist's memorable phrase, 'the patron saint of the proletariat'.

Two golden statues of Prometheus – two completely opposed political emblems. They are (literally) shining examples of what we have seen to be the central characteristic of myth, today as well as in antiquity: its plurality of meaning. But more than that, they, in a different but no less forceful way than the paintings in the Pompeian house, show how myth works *relationally*. Each new creation positions itself in relation to previous articulations of the myth. Each work of art is not only influenced by its predecessors, but in turn impacts upon and changes them. Manship's emblem of capitalism is transformed when one has seen Harrison's film, even if this wasn't the screenwriter's intention (the sculpture is not mentioned in Harrison's essay). Classical myth was – and is – a continuing event: a *process* rather than a product.

Chapter 3
Gods and heroes

Polytheism and morality

The sexual conquest of a mortal woman by a god usually resulted in the birth of heroes. Europa gave birth to three: Minos, Rhadamanthys, and Sarpedon. In Aeschylus' play *Europa* (of which only fragments survive), he presents Europa as a mother who misses and worries about her adult sons, especially Sarpedon, who is fighting in the Trojan War:

> It is for Sarpedon that I fear, that rampaging with his spear
> He might go too far and suffer hideously.
> For this hope of mine is slim and balanced upon a razor's edge –
> I might see everything slip away at the bloody death of my son.

Her worries are likely to have been well founded. Sarpedon's 'bloody death' is one of the most climactic scenes in Homer's *Iliad* and reveals much about heroes – and gods – in classical mythology. In book 16 of the epic poem, Sarpedon, a fighter on the Trojan side of the war, comes head to head with the Greek warrior Patroclus. Unusually, in the *Iliad*, Sarpedon's mother is a woman called Laodamia, not Europa, but the emphasis in any case is on the hero's relationship with his father, Zeus. Observing the action from the safety of Mount Olympus, Zeus realizes that his son is in trouble. Lamenting the unkindness of Fate, the god acknowledges that it is Sarpedon's destiny to be killed by Patroclus. His dilemma is whether or not to intervene and save his son: 'I am in two minds', he says to his wife, Hera. 'Shall I snatch him up and set him down alive ... or shall I let him fall?' Hera is indignant. She points out that to intervene would be the thin end of the wedge; if *he* saves his son then *all* of the gods will expect their sons to be saved. Zeus concedes, 'but he wept tears of blood that streamed to the ground, honouring his beloved son'.

This scene is remarkable for its portrayal of power and causality. It presents a world in which it is not entirely clear who or what is ultimately responsible for the causation of events in the world. Events are allotted by Fate, but not, it seems, immutably. Zeus implies that he has the power to change Fate, but this remains theoretical. Nor is it clear where human agency fits into this order. The first lines of the poem suggest that events are doubly determined, by both the anger of Achilles, and the plan of Zeus. Is the death of Sarpedon part of the plan of Zeus? And why does the lord of the gods behave feebly when faced with the possibility of protest from the others? Is it self-sacrifice or moral abnegation for Zeus to abandon his son in order to avoid trouble?

Although configurations of Zeus vary in different authors, images, and religious practices, Homer's portrayal (from which most other representations spring) shows a complexity that is characteristic of Greek (and Roman) theology. Zeus is the most powerful god, but even he has limits on his power. Unlike the monotheistic religions of Islam, Judaism, and Christianity, Greek and Roman religion was polytheistic. Mortals could never be certain they had done the right thing. Being completely obedient to and favoured by one god wouldn't protect a mortal from the wrath of another god. There was no good or evil in Greek and Roman religion, and few mythological characters were wholly bad or wholly good. Nor was there any single religious text, like the Bible or Koran, which laid down for people a moral code to follow. Faith was not defined

against disbelief as it is in most modern religions. In fact, ↳
in terms of 'religion' as a separate part of life is misleading; th
gods were involved in every sphere of activity.

Modern books on classical myth often introduce the pantheon of
principal deities with a table like this:

Greek name (Roman name)	Concern	Attributes
Zeus (Jupiter, Jove)	kingship; oaths; law; weather	thunderbolt; sceptre; eagle
Hera (Juno)	marriage; family	crown; peacock
Poseidon (Neptune)	sea; earthquakes	trident; dolphins
Hades (Pluto, Dis)	lord of the Underworld	cap of invisibility; sceptre
Demeter (Ceres)	harvest; fertility	grain
Aphrodite (Venus)	love; sex	doves; Eros
Hestia (Vesta)	the hearth	(rarely depicted)
Apollo (Apollo)	music; healing; plague; the sun; prophecy	lyre; bow and arrows; laurel
Artemis (Diana)	hunting; wild animals; helper of women in childbirth	bow and arrows

(Cont.)

	Concern	Attributes
(Mercury)	messenger; trade; guider of souls to the Underworld	winged shoes; caduceus (wand with two intertwined serpents)
Hephaestus (Vulcan)	crafts; metalwork	axe, anvil; physical disability
Ares (Mars)	war	spear; shield
Athena (Minerva)	crafts; wisdom; warfare, esp. to protect the city	helmet and spear; aegis (cape with snakes and head of Gorgon); owl
Dionysus (Bacchus, Liber)	ecstasy; intoxication; wine	ivy; vines; panthers; thyrsus (wand)
Persephone (Proserpina)	bride of Hades and queen of the Underworld	cornucopia
Pan (Faunus)	wilderness; induces *pan*ic	half-goat, half-human; pan-pipes

Such charts are obviously useful (and I'm having my cake and eating it by including this one), but it's worthwhile taking into account their distortions. They present a static picture of the immortals, one that irons out historical change and cultural context. Apollo's association with the sun was a relatively late development; Demeter and Persephone were intimately connected with the Eleusinian mystery cult, to take two examples. The chart also presents the Roman pantheon as merely a reflection of the

Greek one, just with the names changed, an assimilation that occludes the many important differences between Greek and Roman deities. Most importantly, it underplays the fact that it was the gods' *interactions* with each other, and with mortals, that gave the myths meaning. It was through their loves, enmities, alliances, and arguments that moral questions were raised and debated. It was not important that the gods had moral authority; they did not. They were unfaithful, vengeful, petty, and mean, just as humans are. But it was important that humans recognized the difference between themselves and the immortals and honoured the gods in cult and through ritual, especially sacrifice.

If there were rewards for honouring the gods, and for leading a good life, they were enjoyed in this life, not the next. There is no simple and unified picture of the afterlife that emerges from ancient sources, but what is clear is that there is no equivalent of the Christian categories of heaven and hell. Most thought that the dead went to Hades, an unlovely place but not one that was feared. Various philosophical schools and mystery cults were more interested in eschatology (literally, 'the study of last things') and believed in such things as a blessed afterlife, and the transmigration of souls. An idea occasionally mentioned in ancient sources is that there was an alternative resting place to Hades for a select few. One version was known as Elysium, or the Elysian Fields, another as 'the Islands of the Blest', but these paradises were reserved for the distinguished and well connected rather than for the conspicuously good. Cadmus, Achilles, and Menelaus, none of whom were renowned for their moral superiority, but all of whom had impeccable family connections, were said by some to have acquired places in Elysium. Elysium was a kind of Martha's Vineyard or Val d'Isère for the deceased.

Europa's sons Rhadamanthys and Minos were rulers and judges of Elysium (settling disputes between the dead), although in Virgil's *Aeneid*, it was Tartarus that was Rhadamanthys' realm. Tartarus was either an area within Hades, or a more remote and bleak region altogether, and it was where some of those who had committed gross crimes were punished. Sisyphus had tried to cheat Death; his punishment in Tartarus was to push a rock uphill, only to have it roll back down as he neared the top – again and again for eternity.

Many myths dramatize the disastrous consequences for mortals of overstepping the boundaries between them and us, or otherwise dishonouring the gods. This dishonour, presumption, or insolence was called *hubris*. Prometheus showed hubris when he stole fire from Olympus; Sisyphus when he tried to deceive Death. While out hunting, Actaeon saw Artemis bathing in the nude; he was turned into a stag and devoured by his own hounds. The Phrygian satyr Marsyas challenged Apollo to a music contest; his pipe versus the god's lyre. For this hubris, Apollo suspended the satyr from a pine tree and had him skinned alive, an episode most famously and vividly captured in modernity by Titian's *The Flaying of Marsyas*. These narratives are cautionary tales. Their ideological purpose is clear: they keep us in our place.

An extreme version of this interpretation of myth – that myth is a form of state propaganda designed to frighten and control people – is advanced in one of the fascinating analyses of myth that survives from antiquity. It is found in another fragment of a 5th-century Greek play and is spoken by the character Sisyphus. It's worth quoting from at some length:

> There was a time when human life was without order
> and bestial and ruled by brute force,
> when there was neither any reward for the good
> nor any punishment for the bad.
> And then, I think, men established
> punitive laws, so that Justice would be ruler of all
> <...> and have Hubris in chains.
> Whoever did wrong was punished.
> Then, given that the laws held people back from
> openly committing violent deeds

but they still did them in secret, at that time I think
<...> some man of shrewd and intelligent character
hit upon the idea of inventing the gods for mortals, so
that bad people would have something to fear even when
they acted or spoke or schemed in secret.

It goes on to describe the spin-doctor's invention of the gods and
their landscapes, before concluding: 'He hedged men in with such
terrible fears ... and doused lawlessness with these fears of his ... In
this way, I think, someone first convinced mortals to believe that a
race of gods existed.' It is, as religious historian Bruce Lincoln puts
it, 'one of the earliest, most thorough, and most ruthlessly cynical
theories of ideology – more specifically of religion as ideology – in
the history of Western thought'. The play it comes from was a satyr
drama (a kind of comedy), or a tragedy, entitled *Sisyphus*, and
probably the work of noted Athenian politician Critias (though
others think it was by Euripides). But we must be careful. The
character Sisyphus, one of mythology's arch-deceivers, is hardly
likely to be a spokesman for the playwright, and we should not
take this speech at face value. We have no idea whether the views
expressed by 'Sisyphus' were promoted or mocked. How this
cynical and self-conscious critique of myth as ideological control
was originally intended and understood remains tantalizingly
unknown.

Of course, we need not agree with 'Sisyphus'. For all a mythical
narrative's cautionary power, the very malleability of myth ensures
that the politics of any one version can be reversed in another.
Take the case of Marsyas. As commonly told, the myth affirms
Apollo's supremacy and the dangers of challenging the gods.
However, in the Roman Republic, Marsyas' myth hailed the state's
liberation from patrician (elite) authority. The tale was given a
different spin: Marsyas had not been killed by Apollo, but was
instead rescued by Liber, god of *Liber*ation (not merely the Roman
'equivalent' of Dionysus), who brought him to Italy, where he
founded the Marsic people, ancestors of the powerful non-patrician

10. Statue of Marsyas as a symbol of liberation

family, the Marcii. Apollo represented what the Republic had fought to overcome, and bronze statues of Marsyas were erected in comitium area of the Roman forum (where the political decision-making took place) and in the public squares across Italy. The one depicted in Figure 10 survives from Paestum. You can see the leg irons around his ankles. He originally had his right arm raised as a symbol of *libertas*. This is still state ideology, of course, but one in which the god is criticized and the rebel lauded. The statues of Marysas stood where they had been put up long after the fall of the Republic and the decline of the cult of Liber. The significance of the icon would have changed again over time.

Identification with the stars

It is myth's flexible quality that makes personal identification with a mythic character a high-risk strategy. Its associations are hard to control.

From among the glitterati of the mid-20th century we find a telling example. Figure 11 is a portrait of Mrs Anthony Eden (née Beatrice Beckett), daughter of Sir Gervase Beckett, chairman of the *Yorkshire Post*, and wife of Sir Anthony Eden, who served as British Prime Minister from 1955 to 1957. It was taken in 1935 (when Anthony Eden had just been made British Foreign Secretary) and is one of a series of 21 portraits of society ladies by the pioneering photographer Madame Yevonde for her exhibition *The Goddesses*. The exhibition was held in her studio in Berkeley Square, a fashionable part of London's West End, and was inspired both by the tradition in 18th-century painting of portraying beautiful women as Greek goddesses and, more immediately, by a grand 'Olympian Ball' held at Claridges hotel in London in March 1935, to which London's in-crowd thronged, dressed as gods, goddesses, nymphs, and satyrs. The subjects of Yevonde's portraits are all distinguished women and 'it-girls' of the day. Dorothy, Duchess of Wellington, is a macabre Hecate; Gertrude Lawrence, actress and close friend of Noel Coward, poses jauntily as Thalia, the Muse of Comedy; Margaret, Duchess of Argyll (Mrs Charles Sweeney), plays a brooding Helen of Troy; and Mrs Eden is the Muse Clio.

11. *Clio* (**Mrs Anthony Eden**) **by Madame Yevonde**

The Muses were the daughters of Zeus and Mnemosyne
(Memory), and they presided over literature and the arts: Calliope
presided over epic poetry; Euterpe, lyric poetry; Melpomene,
tragedy; Terpsichore, dancing; Erato, love poetry; Polyhymnia,
sacred music; Urania, astronomy; Thalia, comedy; and Clio,
history (though their number and assignations are far from

consistent). One of their roles was to inspire poets and artists to produce great work. 'Blessed are the ones whom the Muses love; sweet is the sound that flows from their lips' says the *Homeric Hymn to the Muses and Apollo*. Muses in ancient myth played a more dynamic role than modern scholarship often has it (something I shall return to in Chapter 7). It would seem apposite for the wife of the then Foreign Secretary to be cast as an inspiration to the makers of history. However, while her husband was travelling to meet Hitler, Stalin, and Mussolini, Beatrice was, according to his biographers at least, bored rigid with politics. She was 'utterly unsuited to be the wife of a politician', froze when in company, and was deemed a 'half-wit' by George VI. Ten years after she posed for her portrait, Beatrice moved to America and was divorced in 1950 on grounds of desertion. There's more than a whiff of sexism in the biographies of Eden, which blame Beatrice for the breakdown of the marriage, but, even so, it is hard not to conclude that Yevonde, a socialist and suffragette, was having a wicked dig at the Conservative minister and his wife. And what are we to make of the casting of Lady Alexandra Haig, daughter of Field Marshal Earl Haig, as the seductive witch Circe? Or 'The Honourable Mrs Bryan Guinness (Lady Diana Mosley)', whose coy Venus surely reminded the viewing public that her marriage to Bryan Guinness, Lord Moyne, in 1929, was curtailed when she eloped with the British Fascist leader Oswald Mosley. Goddess of desire indeed! Were these women in on the joke, or did they simply revel in the glamour of their immortalization?

Personal identification with a figure from classical mythology was something frequently sought in antiquity too, often with equally dubious results. The emperor Commodus was one in a great tradition of egoists (from Alexander the Great to Mark Antony to Napoleon and Mussolini) who fashioned himself as the hero Hercules. Hercules, son of Zeus and the mortal woman Alcmena, was a mythic superstar, best known for his twelve labours, the first of which, the killing of the Nemean lion, gave him his distinctive club and lion-skin. His many adventures gave him a reputation for being strong and courageous, and he was the only hero who, after deification, was allowed to dwell on Mount Olympus. In classical Greece, Heracles (as he was then called) was a Panhellenic hero, that is to say, he was worshipped throughout Greece.

His myths often portrayed him as embodying Greek spirit and values in opposition to foreign enemies. The red-figure vase in Figure 12 shows Heracles attacking Egyptians who were attempting to sacrifice the hero on the altar in the foreground. Art and literature from the 5th century onwards tell the story of how the Egyptian king Busiris regularly dispatched foreign visitors by sacrificing them on his altars. He tried to do the same to Heracles, who burst from his bonds, killed the Egyptian priests, and turned Busiris into *his* sacrificial victim. On the vase, Busiris cowers on one side of the altar as Heracles is about to smash him with the body of one of his men, whom he is holding by the ankles. There is not one shred of Egyptian evidence for the existence of a King Busiris, or for the Egyptians ever practising human sacrifice; the myth has no basis in fact. It is political propaganda in which the glorious Greek hero, Heracles, defeats the perverted, cowardly Egyptians. This did not go unchallenged in the Greek sources. Herodotus, in particular, emphatically denied that Egyptians would have done any such thing.

Hercules was mighty, but he was also uncontrollable. In some narratives, he went mad and killed his wife and children. Commodus, who succeeded his father Marcus Aurelius as Roman emperor and ruled from AD 180 to 92, called himself 'Hercules Romanus' and mounted an aggressive PR campaign that styled him as the hero. The bust in Figure 13, now in the Capitoline Museum in Rome, is an exquisite example of Commodus as Hercules. Whether it was produced during or after Commodus' reign, it is entirely consistent with his programme of self-representation as the hero. Wearing a lion-skin and holding a club, Hercules' signature look, Commodus holds the apples of the Hesperides (nymphs who cared for Hera's orchard), spoils of

12. Heracles fights the Egyptians

another labour, in his left hand and is supported by a pedestal with a globe adorned with zodiacal signs thought to refer to important dates in Commodus' and Hercules' lives, with two statues of kneeling Amazons recalling Hercules' victory over the mythic women. Commodus' identification with Hercules might have been successful spin, at least in part, but historians

13. The emperor Commodus plays Hercules

amplified the negative associations. Cassius Dio, in his *Roman History*, presents Commodus as a lunatic and excessively cruel. In particular, he mocks the emperor's acting the part of Hercules in the amphitheatre (where scenes from mythology were frequently acted out with a sado-comic twist). Dio reports that he had all the men in the city who couldn't walk rounded up, costumed, and forced to fight in the arena as giants to his Hercules. They were given sponges to throw instead of stones and Commodus clubbed them to death – hardly heroic, Dio implies. Through the cold eye of history at any rate, Commodus' identification with Hercules was self-promotion gone badly awry.

Myth is too baroque to operate simply as a form of social control, or to be used as a secure means of personal aggrandisement. It always contains the possibility of a different meaning, and for any moral of the story to be reversed.

Why Theseus, and not Lycurgus?

What made a hero a hero? We could answer this with a checklist (must be strong, kills monsters, and so on), but we might get to the heart of the matter if we approach the question by asking a more difficult one: why were some characters made heroes, and not others? Why Theseus, and not Lycurgus?

On the face of it, both of these figures had the potential to make it big in mythology. Theseus was king of Athens who unified the villages of Attica (a region of what is today southern Greece) into a single state, with Athens at its head. Lycurgus was the chief political reformer of Sparta, introducing its laws and institutions. Theseus is one of the best-known heroes in classical myth. He is renowned for meting out just punishment (dispatching a number of vile characters, including Sinis, who used to kill passers-by by attaching them to branches of a pine tree and then releasing the branches so they were ripped apart); for besting Minos (who was king of Crete before he became a judge in the Underworld) when he killed the Minotaur and escaped from the labyrinth with the help of Minos's daughter, Ariadne, whom he later abandoned; for fighting Amazons and centaurs; for trying to abduct Persephone from the Underworld; for marrying Phaedra, who fell disastrously in love with her stepson, Hippolytus – all these exploits, and more. Lycurgus' profile is modest by comparison. He is said to have received his laws from Apollo at Delphi, but that's about it. Lycurgus never made the A-list. Why?

The answer that Theseus was mythical and Lycurgus historical will not do. If 'mythical' here means 'didn't exist', then both men could fall in that category. It is equally possible that both characters had their basis in real people; we simply do not have enough evidence to say for certain. In any case, 'historical' and 'mythical' are by no means opposed or exclusive designations. Socrates, Alexander the Great, and Spartacus were all 'historical' figures who were also mythologized. They really existed, but also became figures of fantasy to such an extent that it is impossible to tell facts about them from fiction. Mythographers made little distinction between historical and mythological figures. Valerius Maximus, the Roman author of a collection of anecdotes, discusses Theseus and other characters typically categorized as mythological alongside orators and politicians. In Ovid's *Ibis*, an anthology of cautionary tales of tragedy and betrayal, historical and mythological figures feature indiscriminately. Roman emperors frequently mythologized their predecessors (and hence themselves) by having them deified, a process known as *apotheosis*. Ovid's *Metamorphoses* ends its tales of mythological transformations with the deification of Julius Caesar. Thus the emperor Vespasian, on his deathbed, is said to have quipped, 'Damn, I get the feeling I'm becoming a god. ...' The boundaries between myth and history were far from solid.

The answer that Theseus was better than, in the sense of morally superior to, Lycurgus is no more satisfactory an explanation. Both became objects of worship. 'Hero cult', as this worship was called, was a practice that became widespread from the 8th century BC. But, in any case, if virtue were a criterion for someone being recognized as a hero, then Heracles would never have made it. Nor Achilles. Nor, arguably, 'love-'em-and-leave-'em' Theseus. Many of the heroes of myth were, by modern standards, closer to psychopaths than saints.

What makes someone mythic is not whether or not he lived, or lived well, but whether or not he was larger than life. Mythic heroes were – and are – outrageous and outstanding. They are phenomenal. They distil some collective ideal or fantasy. That's why we can speak of 'the myth of John Lennon', but not 'the myth of John Major'. And it's also why Theseus made it and Lycurgus didn't. From the 6th century BC onwards, Theseus became increasingly associated with Athens and its democratic reforms. His strength, political nous, and reputation for justice made him an ideal icon of Athens' self-image. The Spartans could have done something similar with Lycurgus, and perhaps they did to some degree, but a prior mythical narrative and commitment got in the way. It was important to the Spartans that Sparta be seen as having been founded (or re-founded) by the descendants of Heracles (the Heraclidae). They cultivated myths that promoted their connection to the Heraclidae. As a result, Lycurgus was eclipsed. Whether Lycurgus does not have great narratives of adventure and conquest because he failed to channel the city's psychological needs in any major way, or whether part of his failure to do so was his lack of exploits, is unknowable. But it certainly didn't help raise his profile, and, in the annals of Greek mythology, he remains resolutely B-list.

Heroes were heroes because they captured the *Zeitgeist* and embodied the fantasies of the people. The heroes of classical mythology were figures from the *past*. But what made them heroes, their *mythism*, if you like, always came from their importance to the *present*.

Chapter 4
Metamorphoses of mythology

Plato's legacy

The novel *Leucippe and Clitophon*, written in Greek during the 2nd century AD by Achilles Tatius, opens with the story of an unnamed traveller's arrival in Sidon and a lavish description of a painting of Europa he saw there. Being a lover himself, the traveller is particularly interested in the artist's depiction of Eros leading the bull and thinks aloud about the power of love. The young man standing nearby hears this comment and strikes up a conversation, admitting that he too has had erotic adventures. When pressed for details, however, he is reticent: '"That is a swarm of stories that you are stirring up," he said. "My accounts (*logoi*) are like fictions (*muthoi*)." ' '"Do not hold back,"', replies the traveller, '"I beg you, in the name of Zeus and Eros himself! It will give me all the more pleasure if your tale is indeed like fiction."' The young man agrees and thus begins the story of Clitophon and Leucippe.

Our word 'myth' derives from the Greek word *muthos*. In the novel, *muthos* means something like 'story', in contrast with *logos*, which means 'truthful account'. Achilles Tatius' phraseology here also echoes passages of Plato and recalls the competitive dynamic between *muthos* and *logos* in the philosopher's writing.

The use of the terms *logos* and *muthos* (sometimes transliterated as *mythos*) to refer to different types of narrative has a long and influential history. How these terms have been understood, and how their relationship to each other has been configured, can tell us a lot about how mythology came into being as a separate field, and how it has changed. This is not the place for a history of the subject from Homer to Harry Potter. Instead, I want to focus on the impact of two movements – philosophy and Christianity – on mythology, and on our thinking about mythology. Its interactions with these two discourses are perhaps the two most significant factors (until we come to psychoanalysis, which I'll tackle in the next chapter) responsible for shaping the metamorphoses of classical mythology.

One common narrative that scholarship used to tell about ancient Greece was that its development from the 6th to the 4th centuries BC followed a trajectory from *muthos* to *logos*: from myth to logic. According to this interpretation of history, Plato and the sophists spearheaded the movement towards rational thought and away from mythical irrationality. Myth is envisaged as something essentially primitive. This view was established in the mid-18th century by Christian Gottlob Heyne, a German philologist who was one of the inventors of the modern concept of mythology (and who first coined the word 'myth' as a scholarly term). He argued that myth first arose in prehistoric times, when man was primitive, and he compared it with the modes of thought of the 'savages' of his day. The emergence of comparative anthropology as a discipline, a development associated with Friedrich-Max Müller in the mid-19th century, encouraged comparisons between the early Greeks and Native Americans, with both peoples and myths disparaged as 'savage' and unsophisticated. In the mid-20th century, this approach was still going strong. Myth is denigrated in very similar terms in Wilhelm Nestle's influential *From Mythos to Logos: The Self-Development of Greek Thought from Homer to the Sophists and Socrates*:

Just as in the beginning the surface of the earth was completely covered by water, which only gradually receded and let islands and continents appear, so too for primitive man the world surrounding him and his own nature were covered over by a mythical layer of beliefs, which only over a long period of time gradually receded enough for bigger and bigger areas to be uncovered and illuminated by rational thought.

This ideology of myth has proved remarkably stubborn.

It's important, then, to identify the 'from myth to logic' approach as a *myth* about myth. It's a myth that was first forged by Plato and it's been staggeringly successful. Before Plato, there's little evidence that *muthos* had any consistently negative connotations. *Muthos* and *logos* were flexible terms used differently by different writers. Homer and Hesiod use *muthos* to characterize speech as powerful and masculine. They employ *logos* to refer to deceptive, feminine speech (though Hesiod uses *muthos* of this too). Herodotus, however, uses *logos* to refer to many stories that we would call 'myths'. He only uses the term *muthos* twice in his *Histories*: to refer to a foolish explanation for the flooding of the River Nile, and when criticizing the notion that Busiris tried to sacrifice Heracles. To be sure, for Herodotus *muthos* has negative connotations, but it is not until Thucydides' rejection of the fabulous (*muthodes*), and Plato's polemic against mythology, that myth emerged as a separate domain, and a disparaged one. Behind the latter's polemic is a desire to promote the superiority of philosophy. Plato stigmatized myth because he was worried about its appeal to our baser passions and instincts. It might distract us from philosophy and its appeal to the soul or mind (*psyche*).

However, one result of his polemic is that it occludes the important role played by myth *in* philosophy. Plato's works feature many myths (such as that of Prometheus in his *Protagoras* and about cosmogony in his *Timaeus*), and many stories entirely of his invention have become myths (for example, the 'myth of Er' at the end of the *Republic* and the so-called 'myth of the original androgyne' in *Symposium*). These are sometimes treated as imaginative framing to draw in the reader – a spoonful of myth makes the philosophy go down – but this approach downplays their role in philosophical thought. Myth in Plato functions variously as illustration, as foil, as the embodiment of conventions that must be challenged, and as a means of exploring the inadequacies of language. To say that Plato was hostile to myth is only to give half of the story. But it's that half of the story that has shaped the discourse of mythology more powerfully than Plato could ever have dreamed.

Myth *moralisé*

Other philosophers were quick to respond to Plato. Aristotle highlighted the congruence, rather than conflict, between myth and philosophy. Philosophy, he suggests, springs from men's wonder about the world. To wonder about things is to admit that one is ignorant and to desire knowledge about them. 'So even the lover of myth is in a sense a philosopher', concludes Aristotle, 'for myth is composed of wonders'. He also gave a sympathetic analysis of tragedy, a genre largely dependent on myth. But it was allegory that flourished most of all as a means of defending myth from its critics. Allegorical interpretation – a way of reading that detects another more important meaning hidden under the surface of a narrative – allowed stories deemed immoral to be rehabilitated. Homer's tale of when Ares and Aphrodite were caught in an adulterous tryst to the amusement of the other gods is not a licentious episode that disrespects the gods, as Plato, and later Christian writers, thought – oh no! According to Heraclitus, the author of *Homeric Problems* in the 1st century AD, it was an allegory, either of how strife (Ares) and love (Aphrodite) join together to produce harmony (the gods' laughter), or, to take a more materialist slant, of metalworking, with Ares symbolizing iron and Aphrodite the loving skill that softens it. No impropriety there.

Allegory is unfashionable now, but it dominated the operations
of classical myth in the West from the Hellenistic period,
through the Byzantine period and the Middle Ages, and into the
Renaissance. It was the Stoics who made it popular. This school
of philosophy, founded in the early 3rd century BC and influential
into the early centuries AD, envisaged the universe as a living
being that possessed an intelligence that animated and ordered
all things. According to this doctrine, this intelligence becomes
concentrated into a divine figure called Zeus, or Jupiter, or simply
God. This God is manifested in many different aspects, such as
fire, and can be called by as many names as the forms he assumes.
The names are those of the mythical deities: air is Juno or Hera,
water Neptune or Poseidon, and so on. Etymology was used to
support this process of appropriation. Gods could be explained as
natural phenomena through (often rather tortuous) etymological
play on their names. So the Stoic Cleanthes explained that Apollo
represents the sun, because the sun rises sometimes in one place
(*ap' allon*), and other times at another.

Allegory of classical myths also proved a crucial tool for early
Christian writers. They frequently turned to the Roman writer
Ovid. Indeed, by the 12th century, Ovid's *Metamorphoses* was
so frequently retold that the period became known as *aetas
Ovidiana*: the Ovidian Age. Ovid was a prolific and radical poet,
whose erotic poetry probably contributed to his exile by the
emperor Augustus to an outpost on the Black Sea in AD 8. He
produced some of the most brilliant literary mythology that we
possess. His *Heroides* is a series of fictional letters from mythical
heroines to their lovers or husbands (some with the men's
replies); they imagine passion, abandonment, and betrayal as if
from the woman's point of view. In *Fasti*, a poetical calendar of
the Roman year, myths are told fresh and with political bite. But
it is Ovid's *Metamorphoses* that is one of the most popular and
influential works of mythology in the Western literary tradition.
A stunning poem, it tells tales of transformation, including those
of Apollo and Daphne, Echo and Narcissus, and Orpheus and

14. Illustration from Pierre Bersuire's *Ovidius Moralizatus*, showing the Europa myth interpreted as Christian allegory

Eurydice, and it climaxes with the death and apotheosis of Julius Caesar.

The later Middle Ages saw many 'moralized' Ovids. The painting above (Figure 14) is from one of them, the *Ovidius Moralizatus* of Pierre Bersuire, a rather preachy Latin prose version of the *Metamorphoses* that used allegory to Christianize the myths. The picture presents three episodes in the Europa story: her mounting of the bull, whom she is shown caressing fondly, their travelling over the sea, and Europa's embrace with her steed,

now metamorphosed into a human and kingly male figure.
The artist is unknown, but Bersuire gives the following
explanation:

> This fable is aimed at those young women who take delight in
> dressing themselves up and adorning their persons in order to go to
> the play and other places where bawdy young men assemble ... This
> maiden, Europa, stands for the soul, Zeus for the son of God, who
> becomes a bull to save the soul.

Another allegorical approach reinvents mythical narratives
through a 'realistic' lens, seeing the fabulous as an exaggerated
gloss on historical, and therefore more easily explicable, events.
Gods were 'really' kings, and monsters wicked people. This
approach is known as 'euhemerism' after the Sicilian explorer
Euhemerus, who was said to have invented it. For this, he was
nicknamed 'the Atheist'. Euhemerus' work is lost, but his ideas
were summarized by later writers and have found favour ever
since (and even a place on the National Curriculum of England,
Wales, and Northern Ireland, as we saw in Chapter 2). Strabo,
whose *Geographica* presents Homeric myth as geography, was
a notable practitioner. In late antiquity, the Spanish theologian
and historian Paul Orosius used euhemerism as part of his
attack on the mythical past in his monumental *History Against
the Pagans*, a project that was suggested by and dedicated to St
Augustine. Orosius' work became a Christian classic for the next
thousand years. But euhemerism was a paradoxical approach for a
polemicist against the pre-Christian world, for while it took away
the gods' divinity, it also recognized their existence (in some form)
and kept them in the history books.

So was mythology-as-allegory any *good*? How would we now
rate this particular chapter in the history of classical mythology?
It's tempting to agree with the Epicureans and other critics who
scorned the allegorists for producing strained and trivializing
interpretations. To read Sisyphus purely as a symbol of ambition

being 'an uphill struggle', or Saturn as so-called because he is 'sated with years' seems clever-clever rather than genuinely illuminating. To suggest that the ancients believed that all beneficial aspects of the world (sun, moon, rivers, and so on) were gods, scoffs one ancient critic, is to accuse them of rank stupidity. Where should we stop, he asks: rivers, lakes, men, animals ... and household furniture? Much allegorical interpretation rendered mythic narratives banal. But it would be a mistake to think that because it made mythic stories and figures trivial, the allegorizing approach was itself trivial. Instead, it could and did function as a powerful agent of ideology. This is evident even when allegory was not employed to further a particular religious or philosophical agenda.

Let's take the example of Heraclitus' *On Unbelievable Things*. This Heraclitus is typically known as 'Heraclitus the Paradoxographer' (meaning 'the Compiler of Strange Phenomena'), though 'Mythographer' ('the Compiler of Myths') would be more accurate. (He's certainly not to be confused with the famous pre-Socratic philosopher Heraclitus, and is *probably* not to be confused with the Heraclitus who's the author of *Homeric Problems*.) It is likely that his work was a school text written in the late 1st or 2nd century AD. In it he rationalizes mythic figures like Scylla, one of the monsters encountered by Odysseus in Homer's *Odyssey*:

> They say Scylla devoured passing sailors. But Scylla was a beautiful prostitute who lived on an island with her greedy and despicable hangers-on. Together with these she would 'devour' her clients – and among them Odysseus' companions.

According to Heraclitus, the monstrous Harpies were also 'really' prostitutes, as was the gorgon Medusa, and the sorceress Circe, and the Sirens. The magic of the mythic narratives that relies on their characters having special and distinct attributes is lost as most dangerous females are reduced to prostitutes. This is equally revelatory about the author's reading of prostitutes (we often only look at one side of rationalization – what the rationalizing tells us about the myth – and ignore what the myth might reveal about the subject chosen to explain it). They are characterized as hungry and avaricious and, as the gloss of the mythic surface can never quite be extinguished, as monstrous. The specific examples are used as an opportunity to generalize – the Harpies, we are told, behave in a way 'which is typical of prostitutes'. 'By discarding the overly-mythical', the writer Dicaearchus had asserted in the late 4th century BC about rationalization, 'one reduces it, through reason, to natural reality'. In Heraclitus, 'realist' allegory becomes a vehicle for *naturalizing* misogyny.

Others are much less critical of mythic allegory than the Epicureans were. In fact, allegory is often credited with being the saviour of myth, as the title of a recent book on the subject proclaims: *How Philosophers Saved Myths*. Without allegory, the story goes, Homer and Hesiod would have been censored by critics and ultimately forgotten. There might be some truth in this. However, it also makes mythology sound like an imperilled hostage, with philosophers bursting in as the cultural equivalents of an SAS commando team. This view of philosophy as the active agent and mythology its passive partner risks bringing in a version of the '*muthos* primitive, *logos* advanced' fallacy by the back door. In any case, the distinctions between mythology and philosophy cannot be so sharply made. The allegorical readings of mythical narratives undertaken by philosophers (and Christians) are not just something imposed *upon* mythology; they *are* mythology, just in a different shape.

The real advantage of allegorical interpretation is that it expanded the possibilities for imaginative readings of the well known narratives. Paradoxically perhaps, the reduction of myth to metaphor enabled mythic lore to be *remythologized*. To be sure, this was sometimes done in a very dull way, as the Epicureans complained, but there were also creative and provocative interpretations that stand on their own as cultural commentary, if not as literature. We find this in early Christian appropriations of myth, such as the *Ovide Moralisé* of the 14th century. The *Ovide Moralisé*, sometimes erroneously confused with Bersuire's *Ovidius Moralizatus*, is an anonymous French poem written in the 14th century and, at some 72,000 verses, was one of the longest and most significant medieval texts concerned with classical mythology. The prologue promises: 'La veritez seroit aperte / Qui souz les fables gist couverte' ('The truth will become apparent / That lies hidden beneath the fables'), and the poem goes on to retell the myths of the *Metamorphoses* and to offer commentaries on each one, privileging those that Christianize the narratives.

Let's take the story of Myrrha, one of the most disturbing in Ovid's poem. Myrrha desires her father, Cinyras. She recognizes the immorality of her desire and attempts suicide, but her nurse intervenes, coaxes the truth out of her, and plots for her to steal into Cinyras' bed in darkness while his wife (Myrrha's mother) is attending some religious rites. This she does three times, but the third time Cinyras brings in a light and reveals his lover and their crime. Myrrha flees and prays to the gods to punish her. They answer her prayer: she is changed into a tree. The child she has conceived continues to grow inside the wood, which is cracked open to produce Adonis, who will become the beloved of the goddess Venus. Myrrha still weeps, tells Ovid, and the warm drops of myrrh trickle down the tree.

In the *Ovide Moralisé*, Ovid's dark tale of incest is remythologized in extraordinary ways. The possibility of the tale's being an allegory of nature is acknowledged: Cinyras would represent the sun, Myrrha the myrrh tree, and Adonis the sap that is produced as a result of their chemistry. But the interpretation that is 'better and more worthy of being known' is a moral one, in which Myrrha represents the Virgin Mary, Cinyras God, and Adonis Christ. Or perhaps Myrrha is the sinful soul of every person who receives god wrongly, and Adonis stands for repentance. Or perhaps still, wonders the poet, the story is as Ovid told it. If so, then confession and repentance can still redeem the sinner, and good (Adonis) be born from sin. What is impressive about the *Ovid Moralisé*, is that, in combining poetry with commentary, and in mulling over a variety of interpretations of each story, it encourages its reader to engage with the myth on an intellectual as well as an aesthetic level. Christian ideology is promoted, but self-consciously so, and the malleability of mythic lore and the possibilities of alternative readings are also recognized.

It is possible to see the metamorphoses of myth through allegory as doing violence to ancient literature. When St Jerome advises on how best for Christians to use classical mythology, the metaphor he uses is one of aggressive appropriation:

> If you want to marry a captive, you must first shave her head and eyebrows, shave the hair on her body and cut her nails, so must it be done with profane literature, after having removed all that was earthly and idolatrous, unite with her and make her fruitful for the lord.

Some of the Stoic and Christian material, as well as the mythography of Heraclitus, might fit this image. However, I have also argued for allegory's positive effects. It is a process that typically takes control away from the author of a narrative and gives it to the reader. It is the reader who decides whether to interpret writing on a literal or a symbolic level. In giving greater control to the reader, allegory allows for imaginative and reflective analyses of mythology, and for its ideological purposes to be criticized, as well as affirmed.

Myth-as-allegory depended on the idea that myth contained some kind of truth, some important *logos*, if you like. However, the modern construct of myth, shaped by Heyne's notion of myth as primitive and lacking in *logos*, was not conducive to allegory. The theory that myth was primitive and that history saw an evolution 'from myth to logic', a theory propagated by comparative anthropology, resulted in the decline in allegorical interpretations of myth. Psychoanalysis, the next big agent of change for classical mythology, was to challenge this anew. But that's a subject that deserves a chapter of its own.

Chapter 5
On the analyst's couch

'He who knew the famous riddle ...'

In 1906, on the occasion of his 50th birthday, Sigmund Freud,
Viennese neurologist and founder of psychoanalysis, was
presented by a group of his supporters with a bronze medallion.
On one side was engraved a portrait of Freud, in profile. On the
other, an image of the mythic hero Oedipus, facing the Sphinx. To
the right of Oedipus appears a line in Greek: 'He who knew the
famous riddle and was a most powerful man.'

The Greek, a quotation from the ancient Greek play *Oedipus the
King* by Sophocles, refers to Oedipus. A descendant of Europa's
brother Cadmus, Oedipus destroyed the Sphinx, a monstrous
woman-lion-bird who was terrorizing the city of Thebes, when
he solved her riddle: 'Which creature in the morning goes on
four feet, at midday on two, and in the evening upon three?' The
answer is 'Man' (who in the morning of life crawls on all fours, in
mid-life walks on two feet, and in the twilight of his years uses a
'third foot', a cane). So it was that he 'knew the famous riddle' and,
when given leadership of Thebes by the grateful city, became 'a
most powerful man'.

But the inscription, of course, also describes Freud. Two riddles
fascinated Freud. The first, for which he is less well known, was

how to account for the power of myth, especially as told in Greek tragedies, to move a modern audience. The second was that of the mind, how it worked and why it sometimes went wrong. In 1927, in the postscript to his book *The Question of Lay Analysis*, he wrote: 'In my youth I felt an overpowering need to understand something of the riddles of the world in which we live and perhaps even to contribute something to their solution.' His answers, which, as we shall see, were in no small part influenced by classical mythology, and which involved ideas such as that humans have 'unconscious' and 'subconscious' parts of the mind and that we sometimes repress our sexual desires, were so influential that they made Freud one of the most powerful men of the 20th century.

Psychoanalysis and Greek mythology are two sides of the same medallion. To put it differently: without classical mythology, there would be no psychoanalysis. If that seems like too bold a statement, this chapter aims to show that it is not. It will look at the dynamic relationship forged between psychoanalysis and classical myth, and the impacts, positive and negative, that each has made upon the other. There are numerous psychoanalytic theorists, but Freud necessarily takes centre stage. Like many in 19th-century Germany, Freud was passionate about ancient Greece and its myths. He was both an analyst of the psyche, or mind (using Greek myth) and of Greek myth (using the psyche). As a result, he initiated a radical new method of enquiry, psychoanalysis, and wrote a momentous chapter in the history of classical mythology.

Know thyself

Freud used classical myths throughout his writings as points of comparison and reference, but only three are discussed at any length: Oedipus, Prometheus, and Medusa. Freud's interpretation of the Prometheus myth, involving as it does the hypothesis that in order to gain control of fire men had to renounce what he described as the 'homosexually-tinged desire to put it out with a stream of urine' failed to gain credibility within the psychoanalytic profession and is probably best forgotten. His interpretation of the decapitated head of the female gorgon Medusa is brief but proved influential. In essence, Freud (and others) suggested that the snaky-haired head, which had the power to petrify those who looked upon it, symbolized female genitalia and men's fear of them. But it is Freud's analysis of Oedipus that made the greatest impact.

In Sophocles' *Oedipus the King*, which, largely thanks to Freud, has become the most prominent version of the myth, Oedipus has been sovereign of Thebes for many peaceful years, when a plague threatens the city. The Thebans consult an oracle, which replies that the plague will cease when the murderer of Laius has been driven from the land. The action of the play, taut with tension and irony, consists of the slow revelation that it is in fact Oedipus himself who is the murderer of Laius. We learn that Laius had been the previous ruler of Thebes, and when he and his wife Jocasta were expecting a baby boy, an oracle had warned them that the unborn child would one day murder his father. The couple exposed the baby to die, but, unbeknown to them, he was rescued and given to the king and queen of Corinth, who brought him up. When a young man, Oedipus consulted the oracle and was warned to avoid his homeland since he was destined to murder his father and marry his mother. Thinking he was following the oracle's advice, but not knowing that Thebes rather than Corinth was his homeland, Oedipus left Corinth to go to Thebes. On the way, he got into a fight with a man on the road to Thebes (whom he later learns is his real father, Laius) and slew him. He then arrived at Thebes, where he conquered the Sphinx and was offered the kingdom and Jocasta's hand in marriage. Unwittingly, therefore, Oedipus had fulfilled the prophecy: he had married his mother and killed his father. When this is finally revealed, Jocasta is unable to bear the knowledge and hangs herself. Oedipus, realizing that he himself is the sickness at the heart of Thebes, gouges out his eyes and leaves the city. The oracle's predictions had all come true.

The play dramatizes a recurring concern in Greek tragedy's treatments of the mythic narratives: the profound importance of self-knowledge. *Gnothi Seauton*: the motto emblazoned on Apollo's temple at Delphi. *Gnothi Seauton*: 'Know Thyself'.

Freud saw the analyst as an Oedipus figure: a seeker of self-knowledge and knowledge of others, no matter what the cost. The *process* of the mythic narrative was important: he saw psychoanalysis, like myth, as driven by an inexorable movement towards truth.

Freud's relationship with Oedipus was intense and empathetic. He even, on occasion, called his daughter Anna by the name of Oedipus' daughter, Antigone. Today's visitor to his beautifully preserved rooms in what is now the Freud Museum at Berggasse 19, Vienna, is given a powerful sense of how Freud must have worked, as the writer Hilda Doolittle (H. D.) put it, 'like a curator in a museum, surrounded by his priceless collection of Greek, Egyptian and Chinese treasures'. From their place on the couch, his patients would have seen a reproduction of the painting *Oedipus and the Sphinx* by Jean-Auguste-Dominique Ingres. The Ingres painting inspired the design for the birthday medallion. It was also the model for a personal bookplate designed for Freud a few years later (shown in Figure 15). A version of the same image of Oedipus and the Sphinx was, from 1919 to 1938, employed as the logo of the Internationaler Psychoanalytischer Verlag, the official organization for the promotion of psychoanalysis. Freud's Oedipus became an icon for the whole profession.

Not just the process but also the *content* of the Oedipus myth resonated with Freud. In a line of interpretation perhaps not so familiar to us, Freud proposed that the mythic narrative preserved the memory of a real parricide and incest that took place when

15. Freud's bookplate showing Oedipus and the Sphinx, and a quotation (in Greek) from Sophocles' play *Oedipus the King*. The translation is: 'He who knew the famous riddle and was a most powerful man'

mankind was is its infancy: a historicizing approach that echoes some of the 'myth-comes-from-primitive-man' theories discussed in the last chapter. However, it was another, very different, approach to myth that was to prove ground-breaking. In one of his letters to his friend Wilhelm Fliess, published after his death, Freud wrote:

> I have found love of the mother and jealousy of the father in my own case too, and now believe it to be a general phenomenon of early childhood... If that is the case, the gripping power of *Oedipus Rex*... becomes intelligible.

Self-knowledge is Freud's starting point: he moves from his own experiences and emotions to making a general claim about the human (or, rather, male) condition. The claim, first proposed in *The Interpretation of Dreams*, and later to become known as the 'Oedipus complex', is that, 'it is the fate of all of us, perhaps, to direct our first sexual impulse towards our mother and our first hatred and our first murderous wish against our father'. The self-blinding of Oedipus reveals our deliberate refusal to recognize these unconscious desires: 'Like Oedipus, we live in ignorance of these wishes... and after their revelation we may all of us well seek to close our eyes to the scenes of our childhood.' Freud is here using myth diagnostically, as a tool to explain the workings of the psyche. He reads the Oedipus myth as *evidence* of male infantile sexuality. At the same time, the insights of psychoanalysis are used to explain the appeal, 'the gripping power', of the mythological narrative.

In a later work, *The Question of Lay Analysis*, Freud aims to persuade people that psychoanalysts do not need a medical training; rather, branches of knowledge remote from medicine, such as classical mythology, are more useful. In the course of his discussion, he elaborates upon the diagnostic role of ancient myth. Boys, he observes, are often afraid of being castrated. In case we might question the validity of this insight, or put the observation down to 'the disordered imagination of the analysts', mythology is on hand to back it up. Remember from your schooldays, says Freud, the myth of how the god Cronos castrated his father Uranus and was, in turn, castrated by his son Zeus. Myth is here used to make familiar and to legitimate the far-fetched observations of the analyst. Freud's wording here is particularly telling: 'And here again', he writes, 'mythology may give you the courage to believe psycho-analysis.'

Freud reads myths as case studies, from which he draws conclusions about men's universal experiences. For Freud, Oedipus is a paradigm of what all men experience psychically. Sophocles' Oedipus, in contrast, is very far from being a paradigm of universal experience: he is a unique character with a uniquely horrendous fate. He is Oedipus *Tyrannos*, usually translated Oedipus *the King*, which fails to capture the negative connotations of the word. In Sophocles' Athens, a *tyrannos*, or sole ruler, was an anathema to a city that promoted democracy. His Oedipus was an example of the dangers of a different political system, rather than of every man's behaviours or desires. In Sophocles, Oedipus is only a paradigm insofar as his tragic downfall illustrates that happiness eludes mortal men: 'Having your fate, your fate as an example, O wretched Oedipus,' sing the chorus, 'I count nothing blessed in the lives of men.' Freud doesn't get the myth wrong: he rewrites it. He is as compelling a myth-maker as Sophocles ever was.

To be sure, psychoanalysis was born, in part, from neuroscience, in which Freud was trained. But it was classical mythology that provided the crucial inspiration, scaffolding, and legitimation of fundamental psychoanalytic theory.

What if psychoanalysis had chosen another myth?

The claim that psychoanalysis makes, to be able to interpret the mind, to be able to say 'this is how things are', is what prompted the philosopher Wittgenstein to call the practice itself 'a powerful mythology'. Psychoanalysis is often remarkably unreflective about its own biases. So it's worth asking: how might things have been different – for psychoanalysis and for classical mythology – had Freud selected another myth through which to explain the workings of the psyche?

Antigone is the figure most commonly chosen by post-Freudians to recline on the analyst's couch instead of Oedipus. Daughter of Oedipus and Jocasta (and so also Oedipus' half-sister), Antigone too was the subject of a play by Sophocles. In the drama she opposes her uncle Creon, who has become ruler of Thebes after Oedipus' departure. Creon refuses to let Antigone's brother be buried because he was a traitor to the city; she opposes her uncle and fights for religious rites for her brother. This mythic narrative pits woman against man; religion against the law; family loyalty against civic duty; and the individual against the state.

Post-Freudian psychoanalysts Jacques Lacan and Luce Irigaray, as well as critics from George Steiner to Judith Butler, have all turned to the Antigone myth. Two points of substance emerge from these discussions. First, the Antigone myth is more explicitly concerned with ethical problems than that of Oedipus. It is not clear, in Sophocles' version at least, who is right and who is wrong: Creon or Antigone. Had Freud focused on Antigone rather than Oedipus, psychoanalysis would most probably have paid more attention to the *politics* of the developing psyche. In other words, it wouldn't all be about impulses and drives, but also about ethics and responsibilities.

Second, had Freud taken Antigone, rather than Oedipus, as his point of departure, psychoanalysis might have paid more attention to understanding the developing *female* psyche. Because Freud's Oedipus myth envisages male and female behaviour as different (man solves riddles, woman is desired, and so on), and because it presents these behaviours as innate, it naturalizes gender *inequality*. In fact, woman is of little interest to Freud in his

'Oedipus complex'. He is entirely silent about Jocasta's suicide, an important part of the myth for Sophocles. The Antigone story could have provided a much more positive model of female behaviour. There is a long tradition of reading Antigone as a strong and radical figure: a freedom fighter and a heroine.

Another myth that Freud could have chosen is that of Cupid and Psyche. It is obviously rich material for psychoanalysis: it is a story of the relationship between Cupid, the god of love, and Psyche, a mortal woman whose name means 'soul'. The myth survives in a Latin novel written in the 2nd century AD by the North African writer Apuleius, called *Metamorphoses* or, perhaps, *The Golden Ass*. It is a long and complicated narrative told within another long and complicated narrative, so a few highlights will have to suffice here. Psyche was the youngest and most beautiful of three daughters. She was so beautiful that people called her the new Venus. This angered the real Venus, the goddess of love, who sent her son Cupid to Psyche with orders to make her fall in love with the most miserable of men. But when Cupid sees Psyche, he falls in love with her. Psyche is borne by the wind to a palace, where Cupid visits her at night illicitly, unbeknown to Venus and in darkness, so that Psyche never sees him. Cupid tells Psyche that she must promise never to attempt to see him or to speak about their love. If she breaks her promise, he will leave her. Psyche's sisters encourage her to break this promise, suggesting that Cupid might be a monster, so Psyche takes a lamp and a knife and, when Cupid is asleep, she looks at her lover. She falls in love with him at the same moment that a drop of hot oil from the lamp awakes Cupid. As promised, he leaves her, and the rest of the myth concerns Psyche's journey back to him, confronting his mother Venus on the way. In the end, Psyche is made immortal, and she and Cupid marry and give birth to a daughter named Pleasure.

For psychologist and critic Carol Gilligan, the Cupid and Psyche myth is a 'new map of love' that reveals what Freud's treatment of

16. Detail from Jacopo Zucchi's painting *Psyche Surprises Amore* (1585)

the Oedipus myth eclipsed: the female voice, and the joyousness
of equal love between a man and a woman. For Jacques Lacan,
on the other hand, the myth is not about men and women at
all: it is an allegory of the soul's relationship to desire and loss.
He is particularly interested in a painting by Jacopo Zucchi
(Figure 16) which he had seen in the Borghese Gallery in Rome,

77

and which depicts the moment when Psyche reveals – and loses – Cupid. He argues that the myth reveals that the soul only becomes animated at the moment when it loses the desire that has fulfilled it. This is not the place to rehearse the intricacies of Lacan's interpretation – rest assured he makes much of the placing of the vase of flowers in Zucchi's painting – rather to underline that Gilligan and Lacan both read the Cupid and Psyche myth as revealing truths about human behaviour, albeit to very different ends. Both do so to move beyond the model of Oedipus. And both (like Freud) turned to myth to reveal truth. Through psychoanalysis, myth-as-allegory is championed once again.

Unlike the myths of Oedipus and Antigone, Cupid and Psyche is a Roman myth. Freud's promotion of the Oedipus myth was a significant factor in the privileging of Greek over Roman myth in the modern shaping of 'classical' myth. Had he promoted Cupid and Psyche instead, classical mythology as we know it would be differently configured. Had he focused on a myth from another tradition entirely, a Chinese myth perhaps, or an Egyptian one, the field of 'mythology', and the primacy of *classical* mythology within it, would have been radically changed.

But Freud did not showcase these myths: Oedipus was his focus. And for all of Freud's ground-breaking work, it is hard not to think of the Oedipus complex as an error of massive and devastating proportions. This is because he developed the theory in order to avoid the unpalatable conclusion that neuroses had their origins in the sexual abuse of his patients when they were infants. Despite what his patients told him, Freud chose to use Greek myth as a template for understanding their behaviour. Myth displaced observation. Myth enabled what Jeffrey Masson memorably called Freud's 'assault on truth'.

Freud need not have jettisoned his mythological scaffolding altogether to accommodate his clients' stories. Had he investigated – and here the irony is breathtaking – *a different part* of the Oedipus myth, it would have given him a different analytical model, one that would perhaps have made it less easy for professionals working in the field, and facing the realities of child abuse, to discount them as fantasies. Before he became King of Thebes, married Jocasta, and fathered Oedipus, Laius sought refuge with Pelops, King of Pisa, in the Peloponnese (literally 'Pelops' island'). While he was Pelops' guest, he abducted and raped Pelops' son, Chrysippus. It was this offence that brought down a curse on the house of Laius and his descendants. The myth of Laius and Chrysippus is one in which the sins of the father are visited upon the son, and in which violation of a child results in generations of (what we would now call) family dysfunction. Freud, like Sophocles before him, omitted this part of the Oedipus narrative. Sometimes reading myth selectively can be downright dangerous.

Is this 'powerful mythology' now obsolete?

In the preface to his history of psychoanalysis called *Cassandra's Daughter* (1991), author and psychotherapist Joseph Schwartz writes:

> [U]nlike the newly prosperous bourgeoisie of the nineteenth century who sought to invent roots for itself by appropriating the myths of antiquity, we are now too mature to rely on the Greeks for our narratives. The story of psychoanalysis is not the story of Cassandra, but the story of Cassandra's daughter, a strange, not entirely welcome newcomer on the world stage. We do not know the story of Cassandra's daughter. We have to write it for ourselves.

Are we now 'too mature' to use Greek myths as the narratives for psychoanalysis? Can psychoanalysis move beyond classical myth? Or, looking at it another way, is psychoanalysis, grounded as it is in ancient mythology, in an age when people are no longer as aware of their traditions as they once were, now obsolete?

One answer to these questions comes from within psychoanalytic theory itself, and its offshoot, popular psychology. When asked 'Why are we still interested in ancient myths?', Joseph Campbell replied that we cannot escape them, because they live within us. This idea originates from the work of Carl Jung, the Swiss psychiatrist who for a time worked with Freud. Jung pioneered the concept of the archetype. The archetype is a pattern of behaviour hardwired inside all of us: being a mother, for example, or going on a heroic quest. As we develop, proposed Jung, we activate and act out these patterns of behaviour. Archetypes are psychic structures common to all (the 'collective unconscious') and so give rise to images, myths, and ideas that are also common to all, regardless of geography, class, race, or creed. Patterns in myths – not just Greek and Roman myths, but myths of all cultures – are examples of these archetypes. For example, every mythology has a great mother goddess figure, a hero who goes on a great quest, and a trickster. A Jungian approach would see the Psyche myth as reflecting the archetype of the soul's attraction to love. Whereas for Freud, myth is largely a diagnostic tool, for Jung it is largely a therapeutic one. People who, consciously or unconsciously, are following or not following the archetypes within them can be helped back on the right path by analysing their dreams and their relation to myths. So if myths arise from things that are hardwired inside us, then it follows that psychoanalysis cannot move beyond them.

Another view is that it is part of the job of psychoanalysis, no matter what the specific approach, to provide a connection with the ancient world and to bridge the distance that many of us feel between the modern world and our ancient heritages. Only when we recognize that we have lost our ancient past can we mourn for it, and move on. One crucial role of psychoanalysis is to recover not only an individual's experiences, but also a *cultural* narrative. Connecting people to classical myths, and the ideals within them that can give life meaning, is one way of anchoring them to their lost common culture. On this view, the affinities between psychoanalysis and classical myth, far from rendering psychoanalysis obsolete, are precisely what make it important in a world where people often feel that they've lost some of their cultural moorings.

Chapter 6
The sexual politics of myth

Reading rape

Western art history would look very different without classical mythology. Western art history would look very different without scenes of rape from classical mythology. Titian, Rubens, Correggio, Poussin, Picasso: painting mythological rapes, or 'erotic pursuits' that anticipated rape, seems almost to have been a *rite de passage* for the Great Masters of Art. Whatever other functions these paintings may have had, they typically eroticize sexual violence against women. 'There is no man so ... hardened in his being, who does not feel a warming, a softening, a stirring of the blood in his veins', wrote Ludovico Dolce, Titian's friend, of viewing Titian's *The Rape of Europa* and the other paintings in his series *The Loves of the Gods*. Titian's Europa, unlike, say, Zuccharelli's nonchalant rider, appears terrified, desperate, violated. 'Beauty personified' gushes Dolce, and he compares the experience of looking at her to that of the man in Lucian's *Imagines*, a dialogue about beauty written in Greek in the 2nd century AD, who was so aroused by a statue of Aphrodite that he attempted to have sex with it. 'Classical' and 'mythological' have long served as alibis for Western art's enjoyment of the sexual violation of women. In turn, the grand tradition of such art has contributed to the prevalent view that ancient Greece and Rome were pornotopias.

Was rape similarly glorified in ancient representations of the myths? The photo in Figure 17 is of a spectacular and beautifully preserved Roman floor mosaic. The mosaic was originally from Italica, a Roman town not far from modern Seville. We know little about what its original context would have been. Discovered in 1914, it was purchased soon after its excavation by the Countess of Lebrija, who had it, and others from the site, installed in her stately home in Seville in the interests (she said) of conservation. Since July 2003, the palace has been open to the public on a regular basis, and the mosaic can be seen there now, in the central patio, by the visitor determined enough to tramp the Seville backstreets in search of the palace entrance. The mosaic has 25 medallions linked by a cord design: 12 with stars or flowers in their centres, four in the corners with allegories of the seasons,

17. The floor mosaic from Italica

and nine others with figures or scenes that appear to be connected by the theme of sexual conquest. Trying to understand the mosaic gives us a good example of some of the complexities involved in reading rape in classical myth.

The cameos have been identified as follows:

	Danaë and Jupiter (as a shower of gold)	
Callisto (a nymph metamorphosed into a bear after sex with Jupiter) and Arcas (her son by the god)		A personification of a river, possibly the Nile, or the local river Guadalquivir
The boy Ganymede with his 'seducer' Jupiter, in the form of an eagle	Pan, or the cyclops Polyphemus, with pan-pipes	Io, priestess of Hera, transformed into a white cow after Jupiter had sex with her
Europa and Jupiter (in the form of a bull)		Antiope trying to resist the advances of Jupiter, who is in the guise of a satyr
	Leda and Jupiter (in the form of a swan)	

The physical arrangement of the mosaic, with the cameos encircling a central roundel, encourages the viewer to supply a theme or narrative to make the whole composition cohere. The prominence of the central roundel and its close-up portrait perspective, in contrast to the full-length figures portrayed, suggests it might be the key to interpreting the composition. But we simply have no idea who the pipe-player is. The museum's website identifies Pan. The guidebook written in 1920 by the Countess herself claims it's a young Cyclops, a giant with an eye in the middle of his forehead, and 'an endearingly cheerful face'. Others have speculated that it is a specific Cyclops – Polyphemus, the narrator of one of Theocritus' 3rd-century BC poems – and that the cameos depict the tales he sings. But the detail on the figure's forehead looks nothing like an eye. Still others suggest it's the god Apollo (and argue that Antiope and Jupiter are in fact Apollo and Daphne). Each of these different identifications would frame the episodes – and how we read the sexual relations in them – rather differently.

And how are we to think about the liaisons depicted? The mosaic appears to be of 'the rapes of Zeus' or, as the artist Correggio later entitled his quartet of paintings of the god with Danaë, Io, Ganymede, and Leda, 'The Loves of Jupiter'. And therein lies the problem. Are these rapes or love affairs? 'The-rape-of-Europa' has become shorthand for referring to Europa's story, but, as we have seen, different writers and artists, in antiquity and thereafter, represent Europa's narrative with very different emphases, suggesting different degrees of resistance or complicity on the girl's part. This makes it especially difficult to talk about the myth as a composite, divorced from any one individual version. Was she raped, or was she seduced? Well, it depends … (And could a mortal have refused Jupiter in any case, we may well ask.) It's entertaining to spot the dodges used by classicists to get around the problem. They typically take refuge in archaisms: 'she was ravished' or 'he took her'. My rather inelegant 'had sex with' is no less hesitant.

The inadequacy of language here reflects a deeper problem: 'rape' in our commonly accepted, though not uncontroversial, sense of the word (sexual intercourse without the woman's consent) did not exist as a concept in classical antiquity. That's not to say that women were not raped (in our sense of the word), just that it was not thought about in the same way. The Greek idea of hubris would have included what we now think of as rape, but was far from limited to that, as we saw when discussing the myths of mortals transgressing boundaries in Chapter 3. It was not so much the woman's consent that was at issue (although Roman writers in particular did worry about what constituted consent); rather, it was the insult to the woman's father, or other male guardian, that constituted the crime.

But it was more an honour than an insult to have your daughter 'taken' by a *god*. '[F]or the beds of the gods are not unproductive', says a fragment from Hesiod, and to have your grandchildren fathered by a god was a huge privilege. With that in mind, we can look at the mosaic afresh through different conceptual lenses. The figure of the river-god (as the iconography suggests), no longer seems quite so incongruous amongst Jupiter and the women. Rather, his presence can be read as one of fertility and fecundity. Perhaps the sexual encounters would have been read that way too, as more about the progeny that resulted, and the honour those progeny conferred, than about the women's distress, however foreign an interpretation that may seem to us now.

And yet ... isn't that a typical scholarly exoneration of classical myth for representing violence against women? I don't think so. I'm not suggesting it's all OK then, or that the mosaic doesn't – and didn't – also eroticize violence with three of the women nude, or semi-nude, and, in Antiope's case, struggling. What I am claiming is that the formula 'the-rape-of', commonly used to refer to certain myths, especially in art, has reified images (like that of Europa on a bull) as involving a specific and negative experience, despite the fact that sexual politics in antiquity were conceived rather differently.

The sheer amount of rape in classical myth is staggering, and modern retellings tend to omit or romanticize it. According to Roman myth, the city of Rome was founded upon a series of sexual violations of women. Mars raped Rhea Silvia, a priestess of the goddess Vesta, and so fathered Romulus; Romulus and the first Romans (lacking women to marry and create a community, and having failed to negotiate marriages to women from nearby tribes) raped the Sabine women who, after bearing their children, opted to stay Roman wives; Tarquin, son of the last king of Rome, coerced the married Lucretia into sex and her subsequent suicide resulted in the foundation of the Roman Republic.

In these myths rape operates to punctuate moments of political change. But it doesn't just do that. The myth of the Sabine women reminds us of the violence upon which the marriage contract was founded. Early Roman marriage ceremonies incorporated ritual practices that recalled the rape of the Sabines. The Roman writer Plutarch tells us that this is the origin of the custom that has survived to this day, of the husband carrying his bride over the threshold. Many a happy couple today entirely unwittingly emulate the Roman man taking his Sabine bride by force. (Thankfully, the custom of parting the bride's hair with a spearhead, as a reminder, says Plutarch, of the first marriages' attendance by warfare, has now gone out of fashion.)

The continuities are as striking as the differences. Perhaps the most pernicious aspect of the representations of sexual violence in classical mythology is the repetition of the lie that women enjoy rape. It's a lie that is told and retold through classical myth across the centuries. Herodotus' account of the Europa myth is one which rationalizes it, together with other mythical rapes, including those of Io and Helen, as being one in a series of tit-for-tat abductions of real women that first ignited hostilities between Greeks and non-Greeks. During this narrative, he remarks that,

> although the Persians regard the abduction of women as a criminal act, they also claim that it is foolish to get exercised about it and to seek revenge for the women once they have been abducted; the sensible course, they say, is to pay no attention to it, because it is

obvious that if the women hadn't wanted it, they would not have been abducted.

The Phoenicians, continues Herodotus, who remains agnostic (and so opens up a space for the reader to reflect and criticize), disagree with the Persians about this. According to them, they did not have to resort to abduction, as Io slept with the ship's captain of her own free will, and only sailed away with them when she discovered she was pregnant and could not face telling her parents: another model of female complicity.

But the ultimate rapist's charter is Ovid's *Ars Amatoria*, *The Art of Love-Making*. The first two books of this poem advise guys on how to get their girls, taking inspiration from the rape of the Sabines, the rape of Hilaira and Phoebe, 'the daughters of Leucippus', by Castor and Pollux, and the rape of Deidamia by Achilles, to conclude:

> It's alright to use force – force of that sort goes down well with girls: what in fact they love to give up, they'd often rather have stolen … the girl who could have been forced, yet somehow escaped unscathed, may feign delight, but in fact feels sadly let down.

One of the most recent adaptations of the myth of the rape of the Sabine women, MGM's 'Love-Makin' Musical', *Seven Brides for Seven Brothers*, carries on the Ovidian message. The film was released in 1954 at the height of the Cold War, when Hollywood showed that American men were men (and American women were susceptible to Stockholm syndrome). The musical was based on the short story *The Sobbin' Women* by Stephen Vincent Benét. It transports the rape of the Sabines into 1850s Oregon, but is quite explicit about its debt to the Roman myth. Howard Keel, the film's star, sings of how Plutarch told of the abduction of the Sabines, the 'Sobbin' Women' of the song's refrain, and urges his brothers to let this be an example to them. 'Now let this be because it's true', he croons, 'A lesson to the likes of you. Treat'em rough like them there Romans do ...' And, with only a bit of tut-tutting from the film's mother-figure, they do. First performed on Broadway in 1982, the stage version is, as I write, a sell-out at London's Haymarket Theatre and was recently voted third in a BBC Radio 2 listener poll of the 'Nation's Number One Essential Musicals'.

Influential ancient and modern writers use classical myths as paradigms for the view that women just love violence *really* (the Platonic nightmare of the misuse of myth come true). As such, classical myths are powerful agents of misogyny.

Queering mythology

Classical myths also provide rich material for queering sexuality. By this I mean two things: that they sometimes contest (though they can also affirm) the norms of gender and sexuality, and that they allow for the reclamation of characters as gay and lesbian icons by groups later in history.

One of the mythic narratives depicted on the mosaic in the Casa Lebrijska is that of Jupiter and Ganymede. The details vary, but a composite of the myth tells that Jupiter, often in the form of an eagle, snatched away Ganymede, a young and gorgeous Trojan prince, to be his love object and also nectar-pourer to the gods. His family were mollified when Ganymede was given immortality and eternal youth. (The inclusion of this myth makes the 'fertility' interpretation of the mosaic rather harder to sustain.) The poet Theognis, in the 6th century BC, was the first extant writer to see the abduction explicitly in sexual terms:

> To love boys is pleasurable, ever since even the son of Cronus,
> the king of the immortals, desired Ganymede,
> seized him, carried him off to Olympus and made him divine,
> keeping the lovely bloom of boyhood.

So do not be surprised, Simonides, that I too have been revealed as overcome by desire for a beautiful boy.

Theognis treats the story as a charter myth for paederasty, the common practice in ancient Greece of an older man loving a younger boy. The age of the youth varied (though it would have been rare to find him as young as the baby carried aloft by a sinister eagle in Rembrandt's *Rape of Ganymede*, 1635). Paederasty, declares Theognis's poem, is divinely sanctioned.

The story of Ganymede was also hugely popular in Roman art and literature. His name was changed to Catamitus, from where derives the modern derogatory term 'catamite'. It is a myth used to reflect, and so reinforce, social and sexual mores. The visual representations of Catamitus stress his foreignness (he wears a distinctive Asian dress) and his servile status. For a Roman to violate the sexual integrity of another freeborn Roman (man or woman, other than his wife) was a social outrage (an offence called *stuprum*); the Romans were disapproving of paederasty in a way that the Greeks were not. But for him to do so with a slave was perfectly acceptable. In emphasizing that Jupiter's love object was a slave, and non-Roman, the myth distances the god from any suggestion of *stuprum*, and at the same time acts out a (Roman man's) erotic fantasy.

The relationship between Jupiter and Ganymede is a disturbing one to modern sensibilities, not least because its representations resemble what we would call child abuse more than what we would call homosexuality. The myth is a good example of how alien the classical world can seem from our own, a salutary reminder, given that our domestications of classical myth can make antiquity seem all too familiar. Theorists of myth who argue that it is timeless and reflects an innate quality of the human mind have trouble with myths like this one. It demonstrates just how culturally dependent what are considered 'normal' sexualities – and the myths that promote them – really are.

However, it is precisely a sense of the timelessness and universality of myths that makes those that feature homoeroticism such an important resource through which to represent, and validate, the lived experiences of gay men today. The passion of Apollo for the exquisitely beautiful Hyacinthus has a long and rich history as an icon of gay love. Hyacinthus was so handsome that everyone desired him: the bard Thamyris (according to Apollodorus, the first instance of gay love), and the god Apollo. Apollo caused his beloved's death with a blow from a discus, an accident caused, as some versions have it, by the jealous West Wind Zephyrus. The hyacinth flower (actually more like our iris) sprang from the young man's blood with the letters AI AI (alas alas) inscribed in its petals. Tiepolo's *Death of Hyacinthus* (Figure 18) transports the myth into an 18th-century setting (Hyacinth has been killed by a tennis ball not a discus) and exploits its homoeroticism with its focus on the languid male body. Oscar Wilde, in a letter in 1894 to Alfred, Lord Douglas, aka 'Bosie' (a letter which was to fall into the wrong hands and enrage Lord Douglas's father, the Marquess of Queensbury), cast himself and Bosie as the mythological lovers: 'I know Hyacinthus, whom Apollo loved so madly, was you in Greek days…' It was an image to recur, with more poignancy, at one of Wilde's trials for gross indecency. He said to his defence attorney: 'It is only the gods who taste of death. Apollo has passed away, but Hyacinth, whom men say he slew, lives on.'

In two versions of the myth – one ancient, one modern – Hyacinthus is given sisters. These accounts, far apart in time and function, are wonderfully illuminating about the modern investment in queer myths. The first of Hyacinth's sisters is Polyboea. She is mentioned by the Greek writer Pausanias, in the 2nd century AD, in a description of an altar at Amyclae in Sparta where an annual festival in honour of Apollo and Hyacinthus was held. On the altar was depicted the apotheosis of Hyacinthus and Polyboea, 'the sister, they say, of Hyacinthus, who died a virgin'. That is the sum of information we have about Polyboea. However, one scholar argues that she would have had a similar relationship

18. Detail from Tiepolo's homoerotic *Death of Hyacinthus*

to Artemis that her brother enjoyed with Apollo. This implies that
she was part of a myth of female homoeroticism. Other scholars
have gone to great lengths to avoid any such possibility. Polyboea
was Hyacinthus' wife, they say (rewriting Pausanias), or daughter,
or perhaps his nurse. These reactions either excavate a queer
mythology that isn't there, or eradicate one that is.

Indeed, there has been a long tradition of heterosexualizing figures from classical mythology. The first opera that Mozart ever wrote, in 1767, at the precocious age of 11, was *Apollo and Hyacinthus*. It was a commission from the University of Salzburg, and the Professor of Syntax there, Father Rufinus Widl, wrote the libretto. He invented a sister for Hyacinthus, called Melia, who becomes the love interest of Apollo, instead of her brother. Hyacinthus dies but, rather than grieving, Apollo looks forward to his marriage to Melia. Widl has turned the myth from one that romanticizes gay love into one that celebrates heterosexual love and marriage.

So what of female same-sex desire? Here, classical myth is as potent for what it does not represent as for what it does. The myths are largely silent about female homoeroticism. One exception is Ovid's *Metamorphoses*, which tells of the love for one another of two girls, Iphis and Ianthe. Ianthe, however, believes Iphis to be a boy, not a girl. Iphis despairs, and Ovid leaves the reader in no doubt that her passion is unnatural and grotesque. The goddess Isis saves the day by turning Iphis into a man: only hetero love, insists this morality tale, deserves the 'happily ever after'. Ovid's story is rarely retold, but perhaps, despite its rather dubious elements, it will attract renewed interest in an age when surgeons, rather than goddesses, perform sex-changes.

The lesbian heroine of classical mythology comes from the modern rather than the ancient world, in the statuesque shape of *Xena: Warrior Princess*. Originally a character in the television series *Hercules, The Legendary Journeys*, Xena, played by Lucy Lawless, got her own show, and by the late 1990s it was the most widely syndicated television programme in the world, viewed in more than 115 countries. The name 'Xena' in Greek means both 'foreigner' and 'friend', and she proves herself to be both when she fights for justice in a world where the Greek gods are cruel. She has love affairs with Hercules, Julius Caesar, and Ulysses – the interactions between historical and mythological figures are

19. Writing lesbianism into classical mythology: Xena kisses Gabrielle

nothing if not eclectic – but it is her eroticized 'friendship' with the loyal Gabrielle that won her most fans. When they realized Xena's lesbian appeal, the writers began intentionally including sexual innuendo and scenes (of resuscitation, for example) which allowed Xena and Gabrielle to kiss (see Figure 19). In one episode, Xena commissions a poem from Sappho (actually one of the poet's most famous love poems) as a gift to Gabrielle. The level of fans' investment in Xena and Gabrielle is attested by the huge web interest in their 'subtext', which encouraged the writers and shaped the direction of the series. It is an example of how viewer-power helped create a lesbian icon and wrote Xena into television history – and into classical mythology.

Psychic activism

'[Women] still dream through the dreams of men', said Simone de Beauvoir. Take Pandora, who, according to Hesiod, was the very first mortal woman and was created as a punishment for men. Her curiosity led her to open the lid of a jar that her husband told her not to look inside (usually now referred to as 'Pandora's Box'), and she unleashed the evils inside upon mankind. Take Pygmalion, who, tired of 'real' women's promiscuity, made a statue instead and prayed for her to come alive, his very own 'walkin' talkin' livin' doll'. Time after time ancient myth peddles male fears and fantasies about women. Modern readings of classical myth – as we saw with Freud's use of Oedipus – further encode gender asymmetries. Feminist writers, artists, philosophers, and theorists have all engaged with this tradition, using a variety of strategies to revise the sexual politics of classical myth. 'I'm in the demythologising business', declared poet and novelist Angela Carter: 'I'm interested in myths…just because they *are* extraordinary lies designed to make people unfree.' Theologian and cultural critic Jane Caputi captures the revolutionary potential of this with characteristic exuberance: 'Whenever feminists engage in energy-raising mythic/symbolic thought and image-making, capable of reconceptualizing reality and changing the world, this is what I call *psychic activism*.'

One strategy is simply to avoid classical myth: to reject it and its gender ideologies. To rewrite myth is to attempt to dismantle the master's house using the master's tools (to paraphrase Audre Lorde). As poet Muriel Rukeyser puts it: 'No More Mythologies!'

But by far the most common mode of engagement has been to rewrite stories from classical myth from the women's point of view. In Elaine Feinstein's poem *The Feast of Eurydice* (1981), it is Eurydice who has the authoritative voice, not Orpheus, and her reflections upon what it is to be a figure in her husband's poetry reverse the typical dynamic wherein it is the man who has the knowledge and power to articulate the truths of myths. Margaret Atwood's *Circe/Mud* poems (1974) and novel *Penelopiad* (2005) give two of the women in Homer's *Odyssey* the chance to tell their deliciously dark and witty tales. In *The World's Wife* (2000), a series of exquisite poems – some poignant, others hilarious – Carol Ann Duffy imagines Mrs Icarus, Mrs Orpheus, Mrs Teiresias, Mrs Midas, and others telling their myths from their perspectives.

Giving voice to the female character can be a metaphor for the liberation of the female writer. Phillis Wheatley is a moving example. Born in Western Africa in what is now the Gambia in around 1753, Wheatley was sold into slavery as a child. Her American owners, highly unusually, encouraged her education (including Latin) and Wheatley became the first African American woman to publish a book and, later, to earn a living from her writing. Her popularity as a poet, both in the United States and in England, was a factor in securing her release from slavery in 1773. She wrote a short epic poem, called *Niobe in Distress*, about Niobe, a woman who, according to classical myth, boasted that she was superior to Leto, mother of Apollo and Artemis, because she had a large number of children, whereas Leto had only one son and one daughter. Leto called upon her children to avenge the insult, whereupon Apollo killed all Niobe's sons and Artemis her daughters. Such was her pain at her bereavement that Niobe became a symbol of grief. It is hard to read *Niobe in Distress*, with its stirring evocation of Niobe's rebelliousness and grief and the gods' cruelty towards her, without reading into it Wheatley's own pride in the face of oppression. The history of classical mythology is also a history of resistance, courage, and empowerment through an insistence that stories can and should be told differently.

Another strategy for feminist myth-making has been to reclaim 'powerful' figures from myth, casting 'negative' female role models as 'positive' ones. So Christine de Pizan, whose *The Book of the City of Ladies* (1405) is one of the earliest and most trenchant feminist responses to the sexual politics of classical myth (including the idea that women 'ask for' rape), portrays Medea and Circe as pioneers of science rather than wicked sorceresses. In antiquity the Amazons were mythical female barbarians who were created in order to be represented repeatedly being defeated by male Greek heroes. They were not role models to emulate. But for Elizabeth Cady Stanton, American women's rights activist in the 19th century, the Amazons were shining examples of women's prowess. Maud Sulter's art installation *Zabat* (1989) registers this strategy visually. *Zabat* is a series of photographic portraits of the nine Muses. Black writers and artists posed for the roles: Figure 20 shows Alice Walker as Phalia, Muse of Comedy. The

20. The novelist Alice Walker as Phalia, the Muse of Comedy, from Maud Sulter's series of portraits, *Zabat* (1989)

photographs challenge the image of the male poet and his silently supportive Muse, content to enable rather than to make art (actually a contested image in the ancient world too, but this has been played down in the modern reception of their myth). They also challenge the prerogative of *white* women to identify with mythic figures. Thus Maud Sulter takes on Madame Yevonde.

It is perhaps the myth of Demeter and Persephone that has proved most compelling for feminist writers, focused as it is upon the relationship between mother and daughter, how that relationship is threatened by male sexuality (in the shape of Hades), and the grief and compromises that ensue. Persephone was said to have been abducted by her uncle, Hades, lord of the Underworld. Demeter was so grief-stricken that the crops failed and mankind was in danger of perishing. Eventually, after the intervention of Zeus, Persephone was allowed to spend half the year in the upper world with her mother, but had to spend the other half in the Underworld with Hades. Mary Shelley, Elizabeth Barrett Browning, H. D., Doris Lessing, Toni Morrison, Sylvia Plath, Joyce Carol Oates: the roll call of feminist rewriters of the myth is long and illustrious. It is an important myth, too, for feminist theorist Luce Irigaray, who interprets it to express the universal condition of mothers and daughters, who are forbidden to enjoy the eroticism of their bond. It is, for Irigaray, a founding myth of patriarchy. To imagine a different social and legislative order, in which women's civil identity is transformed, would involve rejecting this myth and turning instead to Aphrodite's female *philotes*: a different kind of love, 'the spirit made flesh' that would symbolize peace between the sexes.

While there is much to admire about Irigaray's proposal for legal reform, there are also problems with her treatment of myth, problems that are shared by many of the feminist appropriations. It is based on the belief that universally men and women have different, and naturally distinct, sexual identities: an idea many feminists reject as ignoring the role of culture in forming our identities. The view that women are all maternal and non-violent is just the sort of stereotype that many find unhelpful. Rather than writing our way out of patriarchy through myth, as critic Diane Purkiss observes, 'there seems to be a danger of writing our way deeper and deeper into it'.

Irigaray – and many of the writers mentioned above – are treating myth according to the 19th- and early 20th-century view of myth: that it contains a truth to be discovered. In telling myths from the 'woman's point of view', these writers lay claim to a different *logos* than misogynist writers do, but the model of how myth works is unchallenged. Hélène Cixous, in her famous essay 'Le Rire de la Méduse' ('The Laugh of the Medusa', 1975) attempts to change not just the individual myths, but the very discourse of myth itself. Her essay is a foundational text for *l écriture féminine*, a philosophy that opposes the (male) hierarchical structures of language and syntax and urges women to write 'through their bodies': to break out of the constraints of male writing and create a new discourse. Cixous's work has been more notorious than successful, if we are to measure success by political progress. Part of the problem is that if dismantling the discourse means writing in an elliptical and elitist way, it is unlikely to result in tangible political change. Or even effective (for which do we *have* to read male?) communication. Dare we even imagine what a *Very Short Introduction to Classical Mythology* that's written *through the body* would look like?

Perhaps, in the end, it's laughter in the face of classical misogynies that's the most disarming weapon. I'll give the last word to Carol Ann Duffy's Mrs Icarus:

> I'm not the first or the last
> to stand on a hillock
> watching the man she married
> prove to the world
> he's a total, utter, absolute, Grade A pillock.

Chapter 7
Mythology, spirituality, and the New Age

The stars above, the goddess within

The biggest phenomenon in classical mythology today is the New Age movement. This is a social network with no set boundaries, built around a shared set of beliefs. Its goals are to recognize the 'connectedness' of everything and to promote personal transformation through spirituality. Aspects of New Age theory and practice seem a million miles away from the academic study of classical mythology. I suspect that intellectual snobbery has played no small part in professional classicists almost entirely ignoring it. This is a mistake. It's a movement that was built upon, and gains authority from, scholarship on mythology. In fact, it stems in large part from subjects discussed in the last two chapters: (Jungian) psychoanalysis and feminism, as well as from archaeologists' interpretations of myth.

More importantly perhaps, New Age spirituality is classical myth in action today in a strikingly populist and immediate way. Some New Agers worship the goddesses of classical antiquity. Others do not worship goddesses, but use the deities of classical myth as part of 'self-help' guides to improve their ways of living. It is testament to the profound meaning that aspects of classical mythology have in people's lives, right here, right now. We may or may not share in this, but it certainly deserves our attention.

There are two aspects of New Age practice that I want to focus on in this chapter. The first is astrology: the study of the stars and planets and their effect on human behaviour. The second is goddess worship. Interest in astrology is keen among New Agers but is, of course, by no means limited to them: many more people read their horoscope in the newspaper than are able to tweak a chakra. Indeed, it is thought that the newspaper horoscope was responsible for the revival of astrology in the modern world, with the first one being published in the British newspaper *The Sunday Express*, to mark the birth of Princess Margaret in 1930.

Ancient astrology was rather different from the modern horoscope. Its more learned practitioners enjoyed intellectual respectability, and there was a substantial overlap between astrology and philosophy. People would consult astrologers on anything, from the time and manner in which they were going to die to who was likely to win in the chariot-races that afternoon. The chronology of the origins and development of astrology are impossible to establish, and were debated even in the ancient world. Suffice it to say here that the Western tradition was one of many traditions: Indian, Chinese, Middle Eastern. It was Ptolemy, the Hellenistic geographer and astrologer, who first laid the technical foundations of Western astrology in his *Tetrabiblos* ('Four Books'). But the rise in the prominence of astrology was closely tied to the Roman imperial regime. It greatly benefited emperors to have their sovereignty 'written in the stars'.

The image in Figure 21 is an example of a constellation of stars represented as a mythical hero. It is also an example of how figures from other mythic traditions are sometimes wrongly identified as being from classical mythology. The picture and writing are from an Arabic astrological manuscript from the Middle Ages. It shows a constellation of stars mapped onto a male figure wearing a turban and holding aloft a scimitar. The constellation mapped out is one of the 48 constellations charted by Ptolemy and given the name Heracles by Greeks in the

57

صورة الجاثي على ركبته على ماترى في السماء

21. Mythology written in the stars. Illustration of al-Jathi (equated with Heracles) in an Arab manuscript from the Middle Ages

Hellenistic period. Classicists, therefore, have identified the figure as that of the hero Heracles. The fact that the iconography is very different from that typically associated with Heracles (no lion-skin and club) has been explained as due to the Arabs' ignorance of classical mythology. This is highly unlikely. The script above the image means 'A picture of al-Jathi, on his knee, according to how it is seen in the sky'. 'al-Jathi' literally means 'the kneeling one', which fits with the image of the kneeling man. If this were an illustration of Heracles, we would expect the name Heracles to be transliterated into Arabic letters. al-Jathi is sometimes *equated* with Heracles in Arabic dictionaries, but being like someone is not the same thing as being them. It is better to see the Arab illustrator as representing the constellation in Arabic iconography through the Arabic mythic character al-Jathi, than that he or she didn't know their classical mythology.

Most astrologers working in ancient Greece and Italy did not think that the planets (Jupiter, Mercury, Venus, Mars, Saturn, Uranus, Neptune, Pluto, and the Sun and Moon) were themselves divine, as some astrological traditions did, but they did think that they took on the characteristics of the gods after whom they were named. So Saturn and Mars were planets with negative influence, which reflects their terrifying attributes in ancient mythology. The planet Jupiter was said to be the most dynamic of the planets, and the most fertile, which befitted its mythological persona. (Modern astronomy has continued this mythologization of the planets. Jupiter's four largest moons, named soon after their discovery by Galileo in 1610, are Io, Europa, Ganymede, and Callisto.) The interactions of the planets were also explained by the relationships of their mythological namesakes. It is no surprise to learn that when Venus was in aspect with Mars, astrologers predicted an increase in adultery. Ancient astrology, and, to some degree, its modern descendant, are compelling mixtures of science (or pseudo-science) and classical myth.

Jung interpreted astrology as the psychology of antiquity. The stars and planets, he suggested, are 'archetypal images': manifestations of the collective unconscious. Jung's student, Erich Neumann, developed his ideas on archetypes, especially in relation to the archetype of the nurturing Goddess. His ideas were influential upon those who later promoted goddess worship, a central element in most (though not all) New Age practice. New Agers believe that the energy of the cosmos flows from one single source (monism), and that what we call 'god' or 'goddess' is a principle identified with the cosmos. New Age philosophy has embraced the idea that goddess worship originated in prehistoric times, when, broadly speaking, matriarchal society preceded the patriarchal order, and people worshipped the 'Great Goddess'.

One form of New Age goddess 'worship' is that found on the shelves of the ever-expanding Mind/Body/Spirit sections of bookshops, especially in North America, Australia, New Zealand, and Western Europe. Here goddess worship is metaphorical. It is about finding one's 'inner goddess'. Christine Dowling's *The Healing Power of Myth*, Carol Pearson's *The Hero Within: Six Archetypes We Live By*, Jean Shinoda Bolen's *Goddesses in Everywoman*, Vicki Noble's *Motherpeace: A Way to the Goddess through Myth, Art and Tarot*, Agapi Stassinopoulos's *Gods and Goddesses in Love*: the shelves are laden with handbooks of exuberant advice on everything from career dilemmas ('Ask Artemis!') to what to do if you find yourself married to an 'Ares man' ('He's not a big conversationalist').

One person's inspiration is another's emetic. But rather different in tone from the cutesiness of the self-help manuals is actual goddess *worship*, as practised by groups like the Dianic Wicca (founded in California in 1971 by Zsuzsanna Budapest) and the Fellowship of Isis (founded in Ireland in 1976 by Lady Olivia Robertson, her brother Lawrence, and his wife Pamela Durdin-Robertson). The Fellowship's membership is estimated at 24,000 followers in almost 100 countries. In 1993, the Parliament of the World's Religions first recognized goddess worship as a religious movement. It remains to be seen whether the popularity of the New Age has already peaked, but as formal religions lose support, spiritual movements, movements grounded in classical mythology, appear to be gaining it.

Goddess worship in part arose through, and was certainly legitimated by, the work of Marija Gimbutas, former Professor of European Archaeology at the University of California at Los Angeles. In her ground-breaking *The Goddesses and Gods of Old Europe*, Gimbutas contends that the mythical imagery of the figurines and pictures of pre-Indo European culture (6500–3500 BC) reveal that this was a matrilinear era whose major deity was the Great Goddess. She argues that the Great Goddess was associated with (among other symbols of creation and change) bull's horns, and that Europa (and Artemis, Hecate, and others) is just one manifestation of the deity. Europa becomes not a victim of seduction or rape, but a divine female in mastery of nature.

The people's goddesses

Goddess worship is partly driven by the desire to challenge the roles for women in the male-dominated religions of Christianity, Judaism, and Islam. It's not hard to see why the ancient Greek and Roman goddesses provide appealing alternatives to madonnas and whores. These goddesses are powerful in their own right and rarely play ancillary roles to the gods. Athena beat Poseidon in the contest for patron deity of Athens. When Demeter mourned for Persephone, she plunged the world into famine. When Juno was annoyed by Teiresias' confession that women enjoy sex nine times more than men do, she blinded him. Classical myth, through the configurations of its goddesses (if not its mortal women), positively values female agency.

From Gimbutas' scholarship, catalysed by Erich Neumann's Jungian ideas about the Great Goddess, there emerged in the 1970s an international movement of artists and activists whose aim was to 'reclaim' the Goddess for political ends. Figu is a photograph of New York performance artist Betsy whose performance of *The 7,000 Year Old Woman* or on 21 May 1977 made her notorious. Damon appear

22. Performance artist Betsy Damon plays the Great Goddess in New York in 1977

incarnation of the goddess Artemis as she appears in the cult statue at Ephesus (see Figure 23). The original cult statue stood in the stunning temple to Artemis at Ephesus, which was one of the 'seven wonders' of the ancient world, and said to have been built by the Amazons. The temple was destroyed in the mid-3rd century AD, when the Gauls sacked the city. The statue, however, was repeatedly copied, and appeared in temples throughout the Roman empire, from the Near East to Africa, Italy, and Greece. It ~ws the goddess encased in a garment adorned with different

23. Statue of the 'Great Goddess': Artemis at Ephesus

creatures and rosettes. On her chest are signs of the zodiac,
beneath which are clustered distinctive oval pendants whose
identification is uncertain: they could be breasts, eggs, or bulls'
testes. The worship of Artemis was widespread. St Paul tried to
persuade the Ephesians to reject the goddess, 'whom Asia and the
world worship'. In her performance, Damon punctured each bag
of sand in a ritualistic way and so that the contents emptied in a

labyrinthine pattern on the ground. She evoked the Great Goddess in a manner intended to symbolize the reclaiming of 7,000 years of erased women's history.

It was important to the goddess art movement of the 1970s that it was multicultural and inclusive (although it was later criticized, by Audre Lorde among others, for failure sufficiently to be either of those things). Its aim was to transcend cultural and geographical boundaries by drawing on and merging different mythic traditions and emphasizing archetypes rather than narratives. To some extent, and in a way that is much less conscious of its own politics, the 'Mind/Body/Spirit' part of today's New Age goddess culture presents a watered-down version of the 1970s' ideal. In these books and 'tarot' sets, Aphrodite, Artemis, Venus, and Vesta sit alongside the Welsh goddess Rhiannon, Egyptian Sekmet, Tibetan Tara, Hindu Kali, and the Irish Brigid. One result of portraying the goddesses as superficial and beyond religious and cultural context is to knock *classical* myth off its pedestal. This is an avowedly multicultural line-up of *Girl Power*, in which all mythologies are equally privileged.

Even those who are left cold by all forms of goddess worship are likely to have been affected by the death of Diana, Princess of Wales, in 1997. I am not going to argue that she was an incarnation of the Great Goddess (though some have), rather that, both before and after her death, Diana's story has been told as a myth, and as a myth that knowingly incorporates and plays upon that of her namesake, the Roman goddess Diana. Diana Spencer was first cast as Cinderella, with her early life in particular narrated as a fairytale. But with her virginity and then her motherhood so publicly emphasized, she was also given the role of the goddess Diana (who had special affinities with both states of womanhood). The myth was used to disparage her, as in Simon Schama's patronizing comments after her *Panorama* interview: 'Here's the thing about Diana the Huntress ... treat her badly and she'll treat you to a quiver full of arrows, for all that she looks so demure, so white, so chaste.' It was also evoked to honour her, most stirringly in the eulogy given by her brother Charles, Earl Spencer, at her funeral: 'It is a point to remember that of all the ironies about Diana, perhaps the greatest was this – a girl given the name of the ancient goddess of hunting was, in the end, the most hunted person of the modern age.' The response to her death was extraordinary by any standards. She was mourned worldwide with rituals and shrines. So much so that the Archbishop of York called for an end to the 'cult' of Diana: 'We should be careful that she is not worshipped. That worship should be directed to the God who created her.' The former Archbishop of Canterbury, Lord Coggan, called her 'a false goddess'. Diana, living and dying mythically, became as much the people's goddess as she was the people's princess.

Consolatory nonsense?

In his forward to Anne Baring and Jules Cashford's *The Myth of the Goddess: Evolution of an Image* (1991), a book that builds upon Gimbutas' ideas, Laurens van der Post gushes: 'It is the awful, yet at the same time strangely inspiring story of the feminine, still unvanquished and undismayed, which we are called to honour and obey...' If all that sounds very *Da Vinci Code*, that's because it is. The success of Dan Brown's blockbuster shows the attractions the fantasy of a suppressed tradition of female power holds for us.

So is the myth of the primeval Great Goddess *just* fantasy? Like most myths, it has been shaped by different ideological agendas at different historical moments, and the continuing psychological investment people have in it. Gimbutas' archaeological interpretations are pretty tenuous, and there's little evidence for the historical reality of a Great Goddess in the Palaeolithic era. However, there is a strong model of a universal female deity in antiquity, ironically not in prehistory, where Gimbutas situates her, but much later, in the Hellenistic period.

The identification of foreign gods from Greek and Roman perspectives had long been practised. Herodotus, for example, identified the Egyptian goddess Isis with the Greek Demeter. This was a simple strategy that made the foreign familiar. But the Hellenistic world was a very different place from that of classical Greece. Alexander the Great had conquered Persia in 333 BC, followed by Egypt and the Near East. It was a time of immense and vibrant pluralism and cultural exchange. Religions came into contact, and deities from one religious system were equated, fused, or otherwise integrated with those from another, complex processes referred to by the imprecise term of 'syncretism'. Isis was worshipped throughout the Hellenistic world both as a cult religion (that is, with prayers and sacrifices open to all) and as a mystery religion (with ceremonies and rituals undertaken only by initiates). In the 11th and final book of his *Metamorphoses*, Apuleius describes how his character Lucius has a vision of the goddess. She appears resplendent, fills the air with her perfume, and identifies herself:

> I am Nature, the universal Mother, the mistress of the elements, primordial child of time, sovereign of all things spiritual, queen of the dead, queen also of the immortals, the single manifestation of all gods and goddesses that are. My nod governs the shining heights of Heaven, the wholesome sea breezes, the lamentable silences of the world below. The whole world worships this single godhead under a variety of shapes and liturgies and titles.

She goes on to list the names she is given by different peoples, including Minerva, Venus, Diana, Proserpina, Ceres, Juno, and Hecate. But the Ethiopians and Egyptians, she says, worship her by her true name of Isis. Lucius then becomes initiated into her religion. Apuleius' novel is so enigmatic as to make its reader feel uninitiated, left without the key to unlock its mysteries. So we should be careful about using it straightforwardly as 'evidence' for anything. But its representation of Isis is much closer to the modern image of the Great Goddess than any other ancient depiction. It does seem that, in part, the universal goddess is an invention of Hellenistic syncretism.

Recognizing Hellenistic universalism as the origin of the Great Goddess is unlikely to be attractive to goddess worshippers, however, because it denies the link between goddess worship and matriarchy that has become an essential part of the myth. It denies the fantasy of a woman-run paradise before patriarchy took over and ruined the world. Women in the Hellenistic world had more freedoms than their counterparts in classical Greece, but they were far from liberated (in our terms). We should note that Gimbutas talked in terms of matrilineality, the societal structure in which inheritance takes place down the female line, rather than matriarchy, which means the rule of women. Matriarchy enters the picture with the publication in 1861 of J. J. Bachofen's *Das Mutterrecht* ('Mother-right') in which he argued for a shift from matriarchy to patriarchy. This has largely been discredited, but at the time was astonishingly influential. Its thesis was fundamental to Friedrich Engels' views on the development of the family, private property, and the state. It was taken up by the Cambridge classicists Jane Harrison and James Frazer, whose scholarship on myth and ritual, notably in *Prolegomena to the Study of Greek Religion* (1903), *Themis: A Study of the Social Origins of Greek Religion* (1912), and *The Golden Bough* (1922), has played a major role in the modern study of mythology. Freud also accepted a version of Bachofen's thesis in his *Totem and Taboo* (1920).

The other event that shaped the modern myth of the Great Goddess was the publication of a work as seminal as *Das Mutterrecht*, but even more eccentric: Robert Graves's *The White Goddess*. By the time of its publication in 1961, Graves was well established as an authority on the ancient world, through his novels *I, Claudius* and *Claudius the God* (both 1934), and his Penguin book *The Greek Myths* (1955). *The Greek Myths* was both an extraordinary feat of popularization, at a time when myths were deemed to be for children not adults, and a muddled

111

mythography, very much influenced by his ideas on the Great Goddess, packaged as scholarship. Classicist Nick Lowe sums it up best when he calls it 'a sourcebook that for fifty years has peddled ... drivelling fakery to generations of the gullible, while perversely managing to cling onto the status of a minor English classic'.

In *The White Goddess*, the Great Mother is depicted as an inspiration *for men*, not a source of empowerment for women. The Goddess was a Muse for male poets: 'The poet is in love with the White Goddess, with Truth: his heart breaks with longing for her.' In locating the Goddess/Truth in prehistory, before civilization, Graves effectively makes civilization the business of men and excludes women from it. His Goddess is the 'Flower-goddess Olwen or Blodeuwedd ... or Circe, ... or Lamia, ... or ... the Sow-Goddess'. But she is not the mistress of the universe like Apuleius' Goddess, nor the multicultural one embraced by the feminist artists of the 1970s; rather, she is the universal sex-object, 'a naked woman: a woman divested of all garments or ornaments that will commit her to any particular position in time and place'. Graves makes it quite clear that this love is also hate, and that the worshipping poet also despises women 'and teaches woman to despise herself'. He is emphatic that women should not be poets, at least not in the sense that men are: 'woman is not a poet: she is a muse or she is nothing.' She has the choice 'either to be a silent Muse and inspire the poets by her womanly presence, as Queen Elizabeth and the Countess of Derby did, or she should be the Muse in a complete sense: she should be in turn Arianrhod, Blodeuwedd, and the Old Sow'. This latter option takes care of Sappho, who is duly mythicized as a manifestation of the goddess, while flesh-and-blood women should keep quiet and stand by their men. And even *this* causes problems for the poor male poet, who, according to Graves, is in danger of being domesticated by his wife and family and so risks losing his edge. 'The White Goddess', he warns, in a staggeringly self-serving thesis, 'is the perpetual "other woman"'.

24. The feminist cartoonist Angela Martin's view of the myth of
matriarchy

No wonder some critics have responded to the myth of the Great Goddess with derision. Angela Carter calls it a 'consolatory nonsense'. Consolation, she suggests, for women's culturally determined lack of access to religion, philosophy, politics, and academia. Ultimately, that is my difficulty with New Age's mythology. Not that it deviates from ancient narratives, for, as we've seen repeatedly in this book, myth's malleability is an essential part of its appeal and power. Nor that it 'debases' myth, for, like Paul Manship's *Prometheus*, its tackiness is partly what enables it to challenge the linkage between classical myth and high culture. Rather, it is the prioritizing of the self *at the expense of* the collective, the civic, that seems to me most reprehensible.

New Age spirituality purports to promote change – its mantra is 'transformation' – but, in reality, it endorses the status quo. It preaches changing oneself to accept the world as it is. New Agers are too busy with their affirmations and introspections to do anything like take direct action. Indeed, in some books the advice to unleash one's inner goddess turns out to be little more than to bring back the old 'domestic goddess'. Using myth as one's personal charter is nothing new (as we saw in Chapter 3), but when Alexander the Great chose Achilles, the psychopathic hero of Homer's *Iliad*, to revere and emulate, he did so with action in mind. Alexander used classical myth as his 'life coach' and changed the world. New Agers use classical myth to ensure that the spirit is soothed, the horoscope reassuring, and the house clean, but the world stays the same.

Conclusion

It has been one of the aims of this book to highlight that classical mythology is much more than an archive of fabulous tales from the ancient world. The stories, the lore, are only part of what constitutes the subject. Classical mythology only happens when the stories become active agents: when people use them. As such, classical myth is not an object or series of objects to be known. Rather, it is a continual process of telling and retelling, of provoking and responding, of critiquing and revising. It is process, rather than an event. Or, to borrow Mary Beard's formulation, we should think of it as a verb, and not a noun.

I've argued that to understand a classical myth we need to know about its 'ethnographic context' (to use Marcel Detienne's phrase). Which is why we've repeatedly bumped up against religion, ritual, philosophy, and drama when trying to get a handle on classical myth. I've also argued that myths operate relationally: in relation to other representations of the same story, and in relation to other myths.

Above all, this *Very Short Introduction* has been concerned to show the variety of ways – some profound, others less so – in which Greek and Roman myths were of significance in the societies that first produced them, and how those myths are still making an impact today. This might be read as a pessimistic story.

Some of the ways in which Greek and Roman myths operated, and still operate, are disturbing. As we have seen, classical mythology was and is complicit in promoting racism, nationalism, and misogyny. Moreover, Greek and Roman mythologies, long having been promoted in Western culture over those of other ancient societies, have stolen the limelight, elbowing mythologies from other cultures out of the way. Knowing this, is it time to say goodbye to classical mythology? Is it now obsolete?

Well, no. And not just because classical myths tell cracking good stories. As we've seen repeatedly in this book, myth may affirm oppressive ideologies, but it also has the capacity to provide spaces beyond them. In this way, classical mythology was and is an instrument of subversion and a force for change. Indeed, classical myth is 'good to think with', to coin a common phrase, in a whole host of ways. It is myth's subversive potential that has generated so many worries about it and attempts to control it, from Plato's desire to censor myths, through Christianity's insistence on reading them allegorically, to early scholarship's judgement of them as primitive, and to some modern storytellers' sanitization of them.

Moreover, to do away with classical myth because of how it has sometimes been used would be to fail to appreciate that criticisms of the subject are not just made from the outside looking in. Instead, worrying about classical myth, about its influences and responsibilities, has always been *part of* classical mythology. When we think of Herodotus disbelieving the myth of Busiris, or the cynical criticism of myth by the playwright 'Critias', we realize that classical mythology *has always been* a reflective and self-critical field of knowledge.

The poet and playwright Derek Walcott uses a telling image of classical mythology in his magnificent poem *Omeros*, which is a meditation on (amongst other things) history and myth, that is partly set in the Caribbean and makes strong use of Homer's

Odyssey. One of the characters talks of 'all that Greek manure under the green bananas'. It is a compelling image of ambivalence towards the classical myth: it is both muck and fertilizer, both pollution and inspiration.

One of the things that this book has been keen to stress is that it's not just 'Greek manure' but also 'Roman manure' that has made its mark on Western, and non-Western, cultures. That is to say that the notion that the Romans didn't have any myths, or that if they did, they were just bad imitations of Greek ones, is a false one. It is born of the 19th century's love affair with Hellenism and disparagement of Rome. In this, the book's stance reflects a relatively recent movement in scholarship, led by Peter Wiseman and others, to rehabilitate Roman myth. Roman myths were as important and sophisticated as Greek ones. Even if (and here's where I would part company with some members of this movement) Greek myths might be judged superior on the level of lore; might be thought, in other words, to be the better stories. Greek and Roman myths were essential to the societies that created them (even if they didn't always recognize their mythologies as *mythologies*), and they are essential now.

It is myth's continual dialogue with the past (and anticipation of its future) that makes it so intoxicating, and that makes it transcend its individual articulations. The impact of classical myth on cultures outside Europe and 'the West' is a story that's just beginning to be told. This book has offered glimpses of that story: the ownership of Greek mythology by 20th-century Arab writers, the writing of an (Americanized) African slave's experiences through the myth of Niobe, and the challenge of Derek Walcott's *Omeros* all pose the question: to whom does classical myth belong? It is the question with which this book began. I hope at least that we (whoever we are) can 'live our myths' (wherever we live them) more pleasurably and knowingly with *A Very Short Introduction to Classical Mythology*.

Timeline

c. 800–500 BC	**Early Greece**
c. 800–700	Homer's epics, *Iliad* and *Odyssey*
	Hesiod's poems *Works and Days* and *Theogony*
c. 700	Homer's epics sung at the Panathenaea (Athenian civic festival)
c. 600?	*Homeric Hymn to Apollo* (whose author is unknown)
c. 600 onwards	Theseus increasingly associated with democratic Athens
c. 600	Sappho's erotic poems
c. 550	Theognis' erotic poems
c. 500–300 BC	**Classical Greece**
c. 500–31 BC	**Republican Rome**
c. 490–479	Persian Wars between Greeks and Persians
490	Greeks defeat Persians
c. 490–400	Tragic plays written by Aeschylus, Sophocles, Euripides, and others
445–430	Herodotus' *Histories*
441	Sophocles' *Antigone* first performed
c. 430–400	Peloponnesian War between Athens and Sparta
	Thucydides' *History of the Peloponnesian War*
428	Sophocles' *Oedipus the King* first performed
c. 400–c. 350	Plato's philosophical works

Late 1st/early 2nd century AD	Ptolemy Chennus ('the Quail')
	Heraclitus the Paradoxographer, *On Unbelievable Things*
2nd century AD	Apuleius' novel, *Metamorphoses*
	Achilles Tatius' novel, *Leucippe and Clitophon*
	Lucian, including *Imagines*
	Pausanias, *Description of Greece*
AD 180–192	Reign of emperor Commodus ('Hercules Romanus')
AD 218–222	Sidonian coin with Europa minted
2nd/3rd centuries AD	Cassius Dio, *Roman History*
3rd century AD	Europa mosaic from Sparta (on which 2-euro coin said to be based)
Mid-3rd century AD	Gauls sack Ephesus, destroying the temple to Artemis
c. AD 415–417	Paul Orosius, *History Against the Pagans*
AD 347–420	St. Jerome *Epistles*
AD 387–398	St. Augustine *Confessions*
c. AD 500–600	**Collapse of Roman Empire in Western Europe**
C12	*Aetas Ovidiana*
C14–C16	**Renaissance**
1340	Pierre Bersuire, *Ovidius Moralizatus*
C14	*Ovide Moralisé*
1405	Christine de Pizan, *The Book of the City of Ladies*
1531	Correggio, *Loves of Jupiter* series
1559–1562	Titian, *The Rape of Europa*
1575–1576	Titian, *The Flaying of Marsyas*
1589	Jacopo del Zucchi, *Amor and Psyche*
Seventeenth Century	
1635	Rembrandt, *Rape of Ganymede*

Eighteenth Century

1729–1812	Christian Gottlob Heyne, philologist
1752	Giovanni Battista Tiepolo, *Death of Hyacinthus*
1773	Phillis Wheatley, *Niobe in Distress*
1767	Mozart's *Apollo and Hyacinthus*, opera
1789–1793	Brandenburg Gate, Berlin
c18/19	Romantic movement privileges ancient Greek myth etc.

Nineteenth Century

1808	Ingres's *Oedipus and the Sphinx*
1815–1902	Elizabeth Cady Stanton
1820	Shelley, *Prometheus Unbound*
1823–1900	Friedrich Max Müller, comparative anthropologist
1856–1939	Sigmund Freud, psychoanalyst
1861	Johann Jakob Bachofen's *Das Mutterrecht*
1875–1961	Carl Jung, psychiatrist
1886	Statue of Liberty erected, New York
1889–1951	Ludwig Wittgenstein, philosopher
1894	Oscar Wilde's letter to 'Bosie'
1899	Sigmund Freud, *The Interpretation of Dreams*

Twentieth Century

1903	Jane Harrison, *Prolegomena to the Study of Greek Religion*
1904–1987	Joseph Campbell
1912	Jane Harrison, *Themis*
1914	'Jupiter-rapes' mosaic discovered at Italica, Spain; installed in Palacio de Lebrija, Seville
1919	Jung introduces concept of archetypes
1920	Sigmund Freud, *Totem and Taboo*
1922	James Frazer, *The Golden Bough*
1926	Sigmund Freud, *The Question of Lay Analysis*
1929–1940	Construction of Rockefeller Center, New York
1930	*Sunday Express* publishes first newspaper horoscope
1930s	Literary journal *Abullu* (*Apollo*) published

1934	Paul Manship, 'Prometheus' statue, Rockefeller Center
1935	'Olympian Ball' held at Claridges, London; Madame Yevonde begins her *Goddess* portraits
1938	Stephen Vincent Benét, *The Sobbin' Women* (short story)
1940	Wilhelm Nestle, *From Mythos to Logos*, published in Germany
1940–1992	Angela Carter
1950s	Nazik al Mala'ika (b.1922), Abd al-Wahhab al-Bayati (1926–1999), Badr Shakir al-Sayyab (1926–1964)
1954	*Seven Brides for Seven Brothers*, film
1955	Erich Neumann, *The Great Mother*
1955	Robert Graves, *The Greek Myths*
1961	Jacques Lacan, *Seminar 8: On Transference*
1961	Robert Graves, *The White Goddess*
1970s	'Goddess' art movement
1974	Margaret Atwood, *Circe/Mud* poems
1974	Marija Gimbutas, *The Goddesses and Gods of Old Europe*
1975	Hélène Cixous, *The Laugh of the Medusa*
1977	Betsy Damon performs *The 7,000 Year Old Woman*
1981	Elaine Feinstein, *The Feast of Eurydice*
1984	Jeffrey Masson, *The Assault on Truth*
1987	Bernal, *Black Athena* published
1989	Maud Sulter, *Zabat* installation
1993	William J. Bennett, *Book of Virtues*
1993	Aligi Sassu, *I Miti del Mediterraneo*, ceramic mural, European Parliament building, Brussels
1993	Parliament of the World's Religions recognises Goddess worship as an official religion
1994	*Wahlen Gehen* poster, European Parliament Office, Germany
1995–1999	*Hercules: The Legendary Journeys*, TV series
1995–2001	*Xena: Warrior Princess*, TV series
1997	Death of Diana, Princess of Wales

1998	Rolf Schonlau and Gabriele Knor, *Die Euro Kids*
1998	Tony Harrison's film *Prometheus*
1998	*Captain Euro* comic-strip, *Twelve Stars Communications Ltd.*
1999	Carol Ann Duffy, *The World's Wife*

Twenty-First Century

2002	Euro introduced; Europa on 2-euro coin
2002	Carol Gilligan, *The Birth of Pleasure*
2003	Dan Brown, *The Da Vinci Code*
2004	Wolfgang Petersen, *Troy* (film)
2005	Margaret Atwood, *Penelopiad*
2007	*Classical Mythology: A Very Short Introduction* published

References

Unless otherwise indicated, translations of the Greek and Latin texts cited are my own. Sometimes I have given details of specific editions of texts. With more popular works I have not done so: these are widely available in translations like Penguin Classics and Oxford World's Classics or can be found in the Loeb Classical Library series.

Chapter 1

Quotation from an anonymous Greek scholar: text in G. Dindorf (ed.), *Scholia Graeca in Homeri Iliadem* (Oxford, 1975), i. 427, iii. 506; Rolf Schonlau and Gabriele Knor, *Die Euro Kids: Unterwegs in Sachen Euro* (Wienand, 1998); Captain Euro can be found at www.captaineuro.com; Herodotus on Xerxes and the people of Argos: *Histories* 7.150; Siboi and Alexander the Great: Diodorus Siculus, *Library of History* 17.96.2; *Homeric Hymn to Pythian Apollo*, lines 250–1; Herodotus on Europa and Europe: *Histories* 4.45.5; Moschus' *Europa*: text and translation in *Greek Bucolic Poets*, tr. J. M. Edmonds (Harvard, 1912); Horace *Odes* III.27; Martial on paintings of Europa: *Epigrams* 2.14, 11.14; Pliny on Europe as 'the fairest of lands': *Natural History* 35. 37. 114; Martin Bernal, *Black Athena: The Afroasiatic Roots of Classical Civilisation* (London, 1987), especially Chapter 1; Martin Bernal, 'The Image of Ancient Greece as a Tool for Colonialism and

European Hegemony', in G. C. Bond and A. Gilliam (eds), *Social Construction of the Past: Representation as Power* (London, 1994), pp. 119–28, quotation from p. 127; 'kernel of truth': *Black Athena*, p. 84 and Bernal, *Black Athena Writes Back: Martin Bernal Responds to His Critics* (Durham and London, 2001), p. 91; Nazik al-Mala'ika's 'The Lost Utopia' and Abd al-Wahhab al-Bayati's 'Greetings to Athens' translated and discussed in As'as E. Khairallah 'The Greek Cultural Heritage and the Odyssey of Modern Arab Poets', in I. J. Boullata and T. DeYoung (eds), *Tradition and Modernity in Arabic Literature* (Fayetteville, Arkansas, 1997), pp. 43–61.

Chapter 2

Trimalchio getting his myth wrong: Petronius, *Satyrica*, section 52; school exercise on the Trojan War: papyri in F. Montanari, *Studi di Filologia omerica antica I* (Pisa, 1979), pp. 50, 57–64; Terence, *Eunuch* l. 585 ff; St Augustine, *Confessions*, 1.16; Plato, *Republic* 377A–378A; William Bennett, *The Book of Virtues: A Treasury of Great Moral Stories* (New York, 1993), pp. 211–13; lesson plan: David Wray and Jane Medwell, *Teaching English in Primary Schools* (London, 1998), p. 92; Marcel Detienne, *The Writing of Orpheus: Greek Myth in Cultural Context*, tr. by Janet Lloyd (Baltimore and London, 2003), p. xiv; critics of Manship's *Prometheus*: 'sprung...' cited by Andrew Dolkart on the *Today* show, 3/2/98; 'young man escaping...' *Fortune*, 12/36/139; *New Yorker* cited in *Fortune* 12/3/139, all cited in Daniel Okrent, *Great Fortune: The Epic of Rockefeller Center* (New York, 2003), pp. 292–3; Tony Harrison, *Prometheus* (London, 1998), quotations taken from his introductory essay 'Fire and Poetry' and p. 68; George Thomson, *Aeschylus and Athens* (New York, 1941), p. 317.

Chapter 3

Aeschylus' *Europa*, fragment 99, in A. Nauck, *Tragicorum Graecorum Fragmenta Supplementum adiecit Bruno Snell*

(Hildesheim, 1983); Homer, *Iliad*, 16, lines 433–8, 459–60; Critias: fragment B 25. The text is most easily available in Bruce Lincoln, *Theorizing Myth: Narrative, Ideology, and Scholarship* (Chicago and London, 1999), p. 228, quotation from Lincoln is taken from p. 35. *Homeric Hymn to the Muses and Apollo*, lines 4–5; Mrs Anthony Eden: D. R. Thorpe, *Eden: The Life and Times of Anthony Eden, First Earl of Avon, 1897–1977* (London, 2003), pp. 60, 104; V. H. Rothwell, *Anthony Eden: A Political Biography, 1931–1957* (Manchester, 1992), p. 4; Commodus: Cassius Dio, *Roman History*, 73.20.3; the deification of Julius Caesar: Ovid, *Metamorphoses*, 15; Vespasian on his deathbed: Suetonius, *Life of Vespasian*, 23.4.

Chapter 4

Achilles Tatius, *Leucippe and Clitophon*: 1.2.2; Wilhelm Nestle, *Vom Mythos zum Logos. Die Selbstentfaltung des griechischen Denkens von Homer bis auf die Sophistik und Sokrates* (Stuttgart, 1940), p. 1; *muthos* in Herodotus: *Histories*, 2.23 (Nile) and 2.45 (Busiris); Thucydides, *History of the Peloponnesian War*, 1.22; Aristotle, *Metaphysics* A 2, 982b11–19; Ares and Aphrodite: Homer, *Odyssey*, 8. 267–70; Heraclitus, *Homeric Problems* 69, text and translation in Donald A. Russell and David Konstan (eds), *Homeric Problems* (Leiden and Boston, 2005); Cleanthes: H. von Arnim (ed.), *Stoicorum Veterum Fragmenta* 1 (1905), no. 540; Pierre Bersuire, *Ovidius Moralizatus*, Fabula 73 (text in F. Ghisalberti, 'L'Ovidius Moralizatus di Pierre Bersuire', *Studi Romanzi*, 23 (1933): 5–136); Heraclitus: text, translation, and analysis in Jacob Stern, 'Heraclitus the Paradoxographer', *Transactions of the American Philological Association*, vol. 133.1 (Spring 2003): 51–97; Dicaearchus: quoted by Porphyry, *De Abstinentia*, 4.1.2, ed. M. Patillon, A. P. Segonds, and L. Brisson (Paris, 1995); Luc Brisson, *How Philosophers Saved Myths*, tr. Catherine Tihanyi (Chicago, 2004); *Ovid Moralisé*: C. de Boer, M. G. de Boer, and J. Van 'T Sant (eds), *Ovide Moralisé. Poème*

du commencement du quatorzieme siècle (Amsterdam, 1915–38),
1.45–6; St Jerome: *Epistle* 83.

Chapter 5

Freud on Medusa: 'Medusa's Head', *SE* (=*The Standard
Edition of the Complete Psychological Works of Sigmund Freud*,
translated and edited by James Strachey) 18: 273–4. Freud on
Prometheus: 'The Acquisition and Control of Fire', *SE* 22:
185–93; Freud's rooms: photographs and commentary in
Harald Leupold-Löwenthal, Hans Lobner, and Inge
Scholz-Strasser (eds), *Sigmund Freud Museum, Berggasse 19
Vienna. Catalogue*, tr. Thomas Roberts (Vienna and California,
1995); letter to Wilhelm Fliess: Sigmund Freud, *The Origins of
Psychoanalysis: Letters to Wilhelm Fliess, Drafts and Notes:
1887–1902*, tr. Eric Mosbacher and James Strachey (New York,
1954, reprinted 1971), p. 223; 'Mythology may give you the
courage…': Sigmund Freud, *The Question of Lay Analysis*
(1959, revised edition 1989), p. 37; Sophocles, *Oedipus Tyrannos*,
lines 1193–1196; H. D. quoted in A. L. D'Agata, 'Sigmund Freud
and Aegean Archaeology', *Studi Micenei ed Egeo-Anatolici*, 34
(1994): 7–41; Antigones: Judith Butler, *Antigone's Claim:
Kinship between Life and Death* (New York, 2000); Ludwig
Wittgenstein, *Lectures and Conversations on Aesthetics,
Psychology, and Religious Belief* (Berkeley, 1966), quotation
from p. 52. Cupid and Psyche: Apuleius, *Metamorphoses*, 4.
28–6.24; Carol Gilligan, *The Birth of Pleasure* (London, 2002);
Jacques Lacan, *Séminaire VIII, On Transference*, esp. 16 and 17,
in Jacques-Alain Miller (ed.), *Le séminaire de Jacques Lacan.
Livre 8, Le transfert* (Paris, 1991; as yet there is no English
translation); Jeffrey Moussaieff Masson, *The Assault on Truth*
(New York, 2003); Joseph Schwartz, *Cassandra's Daughter: A
History of Psychoanalysis* (London, 1991). Jung on archetypes:
Carl Jung, *The Archetypes and the Collective Unconscious* =
Collected Works, vol. 9, Part 1 (Princeton, 1934–54); Joseph

Campbell, *The Hero with a Thousand Faces* (Princeton, 1949, reprinted 1972).

Chapter 6

Ludovico Dolce, quoted in C. Ginzburg, *Clues, Myths, and the Historical Method*, tr. J. and A. C. Tedeschi (Baltimore and London, 1989), pp. 81–2; Lucian's *Imagines* 4; Casa Lebrijska guidebook: *Lebrija Palace: Description by the Regla Manjon Mergelina Countess of Lebrija* (Seville, 1920); museum guide: Vicente Lleo Canal *et al.*, *Museo-Palacio de la Condesa de Lebrija* (Seville, 2002). Hesiod, *Catalogue of Women*, frag. 31.2–3; Sabine women: Livy, *History of Rome* 1.9–13, Ovid, *Ars Amatoria* 1. 101–134; Ovid, *Fasti* 3. 219–228; Plutarch on the Sabines and marriage: *Roman Questions* 14 7–8; Herodotus, *Histories* 1.2.4; Ovid, *Ars Amatoria*: 1.673–678; Theognis fragment 1.1345; Oscar Wilde, *The Letters of Oscar Wilde* (London, 1962), quotation from Letter 1; Hyacinth and Polyboea: Pausanias 3. 19. 3–5: scholars' reactions to Polyboea cited in Bernard Sergent, *Homosexuality in Greek Myth*, tr. Arthur Goldhammer (Boston, 1987), pp. 89–93; Iphis and Ianthe: Ovid, *Metamorphoses* 9. 666–797; Simone de Beauvoir, *The Second Sex*, tr. H. M. Parshley (1949, reprinted 1986), p. 174; Angela Carter, *Shaking a Leg: Journalism and Writings* (London, 1997), pp. 36–43, quotation from p. 38; 'Psychic activism': Jane Caputi, 'On Psychic Activism: Feminist Mythmaking', in Carolyne Larrington (ed.), *The Feminist Companion to Mythology* (London, 1992), pp. 425–40; Muriel Rukseyer, *The Speed of Darkness* (London, 1968); Elaine Feinstein, *The Feast of Eurydice* (London, 1980); Phillis Wheatley, *Poems on Various Subjects, Religious and Moral* (New York, 1773, republished 2005), p. 53; Luce Irigaray, *Thinking the Difference: For a Peaceful Revolution*, tr. Karin Montin (New York, 1994), p. 95; Diane Purkiss, 'Women's Rewriting of Myth', in Carolyne Larrington (ed.), *The Feminist Companion to Mythology* (London, 1992), pp. 441–57, quotation from pp. 447–8; Hélène Cixous, 'The Laugh of the Medusa', tr. K. Cohen and P. Cohen, *Signs* 1.4

1976; Mrs Icarus: Carol Ann Duffy, *The World's Wife* (London, Basingstoke, and Oxford, 1999).

Chapter 7

Simon Schama, 'Makeovers: Royal Flesh', *New Yorker*, 26 February/4 March (1996): 42–3; Christopher Morgan, 'Archbishop Urges End to "Cult of Diana"', *The Times*, 1 July 1998, p. 1; Christopher Morgan and David Smith, 'Coggan Brands Diana "a false goddess with loose morals"', *The Times*, 23 August 1998, p. 1. Isis: Apuleius, *Metamorphoses* 11. 4–5; Erich Neumann, *The Great Mother: An Analysis of the Archetype*, tr. Ralph Manheim, Bollingen series 47 (Princeton, 1963); Marija Gimbutas, *The Goddesses and Gods of Old Europe: Myths and Cult Images* (Berkeley and Los Angeles, 1974, reprinted 1982); Robert Graves, *The White Goddess: A Historical Grammar of Poetic Myth* (London, 1948, reprinted 1986), quotations from pp. 446–9; Nick Lowe, 'Killing Graves', *Times Literary Supplement*, 23 and 30 December 2005, pp. 7–8, quotation from p. 7; Goddesses and domesticity: Cordelia Brabbs, *Goddess Power: Learn How to Unleash Your Inner Goddess* (London and New York, 2005).

Conclusion

Mary Beard, 'Le Mythe (grec) à Rome: Hercule aux bains', in S. Georgidou and J-P. Vernant (eds), *Mythes au figuré* (Paris, 1996), pp. 81–104; T. P. Wiseman, *The Myths of Rome* (Exeter, 2004); Derek Walcott, *Omeros* (London and Boston, 1990).

Further reading

General

The most accessible and extensive collection of resources on classical mythology and antiquity is the Perseus Digital Library (http://www.perseus.tufts.edu/). Reading Homer, Ovid, and other ancient writers in their entirety is more pleasurable than reading extracts of them in sourcebooks, but valuable nonetheless is Stephen M. Trzaskoma, R. Scott Smith, and Stephen Brunet, *An Anthology of Classical Myth: Primary Sources in Translation* (Indianapolis and Cambridge, 2004). Ancient sources for classical myth, visual and written, are listed in *Lexicon Iconographicum Mythologiae Classicae*, 16 vols (Zurich, 1981–99). See also Timothy Gantz, *Early Greek Myth. A Guide to Literary and Artistic Sources* (Baltimore, 1993, reprinted in 2 vols, 1996). For theories of mythology, see Robert Segal, *Myth: A Very Short Introduction* (Oxford, 2004); Eric Csapo, *Theories of Mythology* (Oxford, 2005); and J. Bremmer (ed.), *Interpretations of Greek Mythology* (London, 1988). See also Richard Buxton, *The Complete World of Greek Mythology* (London, 2004) and T. P. Wiseman, *The Myths of Rome* (Exeter, 2004), both beautifully illustrated. For the use of classical myths in later times, see Geoffrey Miles (ed.), *Classical Mythology in English Literature: A Critical Anthology* (London and New York, 1999); Peter Green, *From Akaria to the Stars: Classical Mythification, Ancient and*

Modern (Austin, Texas, 2004); and Malcolm Bull, *The Mirror of the Gods: How Renaissance Artists Rediscovered the Pagan Gods* (Oxford, 2005). *Omnibus*, a magazine for students of classical antiquity published by the Joint Association of Classical Teachers, regularly has articles about classical myth and its modern appropriations (omnibus@jact.org).

Introduction

CLASSICS AND 'CLASSICAL': Mary Beard and John Henderson, *Classics: A Very Short Introduction* (Oxford, 1995).

Chapter 1

EUROPA AND EUROPE: Eric Bussière, Michel Dumoulin, and Gilbert Trausch (eds), *Europa: The European Idea and Identity, From Ancient Greece to the 21st Century* (Antwerp, Mercatorfonds, and the Fundación Academia Europea de Yuste, 2001); Apostolos N. Athanassakis, 'Europe: Early Geographic and Mythic Identity', *Dodone*, 22 (1992): 283–303.

MYTHICAL ANCESTRY: T. P. Wiseman, 'Legendary Genealogies in Late-Republican Rome', *Greece and Rome*, 21 (1974): 153–64.

EUROPA IN ROME: L. Richardson, *A New Topographical Dictionary of Ancient Rome* (Baltimore, 1992), p. 313.

MARTIN BERNAL: Edith Hall, 'When Is a Myth Not a Myth? Bernal's "Ancient Model"', in M. R. Lefkowitz and G. M. Rogers (eds), *Black Athena Revisited* (Chapel Hill, 1996), pp. 333–48; M. R. Lefkowitz, *Not Out of Africa: How Afrocentrism Became an Excuse to Teach Myth as History* (New York, 1996); Ruth B. Edwards, *Kadmos the Phoenician: A Study in Greek Legends and the Mycenaean Age* (Amsterdam, 1979).

ARABIC POETRY AND CLASSICAL MYTH: T. De Young, *Placing the Poet: Badr Shakir Al-Sayyab and Postcolonial Iraq* (New York State,

1998); As'Ad E. Khairallah, 'The Greek Cultural Heritage and the Odyssey of Modern Arab Poets', in I. J. Boullata and T. De Young (eds), *Tradition and Modernity in Arabic Literature* (Fayetteville, Arkansas, 1997), pp. 43–61.

Chapter 2

MYTH IN POMPEIAN PAINTING: Mary Beard and John Henderson, *Classical Art from Greece to Rome* (Oxford, 2001), ch. 1.

MYTHOGRAPHY: Robert. L. Fowler, *Early Greek Mythography, vol 1: Text and Introduction* (Oxford, 2000); Alan Cameron, *Greek Mythography in the Roman World* (Oxford, 2004); J. Bremmer and N. Horsfall, *Roman Myth and Mythography* (London, 1987).

GREEK TRAGEDY: Simon Goldhill, *Reading Greek Tragedy* (Cambridge, 1986, reprinted 1988).

PETERSON'S *TROY*: Martin Winkler (ed.), *Troy: From Homer's Iliad to Hollywood Epic* (Oxford, 2006).

CLAIMS OF MYTHICAL ANCESTRY: Christopher Jones, *Kinship Diplomacy in the Ancient World* (Cambridge, Mass, 1999), T. P. Wiseman, 'Legendary Genealogies in Late-Republican Rome', *Greece and Rome*, 21 (1974): 153–64; M. Fox, *Roman Historical Myth: The Regal Period in Augustan Literature* (Oxford, 1996).

MYTH AND ROMAN MONUMENTS: A. J. Boyle, *Ovid and the Monuments: A Poet's Rome* (Bendigo, Australia, 2003).

DANAIDS: Marcel Detienne, *The Writing of Orpheus: Greek Myth in Cultural Context* (Baltimore and London, 2003), pp. 37–49.

PROMETHEUS: Carol Dougherty, *Prometheus* (London and New York, 2006).

STATUE OF LIBERTY: Gregory Staley, '"Beyond Glorious Ocean": Feminism, Myth, and America', in Vanda Zajko and Miriam Leonard (eds), *Laughing with Medusa: Classical Myth and Feminist Thought* (Oxford, 2006), pp. 209–30.

TONY HARRISON: Edith Hall, 'Tony Harrison's Prometheus: A View from the Left', *Arion*, 10.1 2002: 129–40; and the essays from the 1999 Open University Colloquium 'Tony Harrison's Poetry, Drama, and Film: The Classical Dimension' published at ⟨http://www.open.ac.uk/Arts/Colq99/⟩.

Chapter 3

HOMER *ILIAD*: Michael Silk, *Homer: The Iliad* (Cambridge, 1987, reprinted in 2004).

MYTH AND RELIGION: Denis Feeney, *Literature and Religion at Rome* (Cambridge, 1998); M. Beard, J. North, and S. Price, *Religions of Rome*, 2 vols (Cambridge, 1998); Giulia Sissa and Marcel Detienne, *The Daily Life of the Greek Gods*, tr. Janet Lloyd (Stanford, California, 2000); P. Veyne, *Did the Greeks Believe in their Myths? An Essay on the Constitutive Imagination*, tr. P. Wissing (Chicago, 1998).

MARSYAS: J. P. Small, *Cacus and Marsyas in Etruscan-Roman Legend* (Princeton, 1982); P. B. Rawson, *The Myth of Marsyas in the Roman Visual Arts* (BAR International Series 347, 1987).

MADAME YEVONDE: Lawrence N. Hole, *The Goddesses: Portraits by Madame Yevonde* (Seattle, 2000).

MUSES: Effrosini Spentzou and Don Fowler (eds), *Cultivating the Muse* (Oxford, 2002).

COMMODUS: M. Rostovtseff, 'Commodus-Hercules in Britain', *Journal of Roman Studies*, 13: 91–109; R. Hannah, 'The Emperor's

Stars. The Conservatori Portrait of Commodus', *American Journal of Archaeology*, 90: 337–42.

HERCULES: Alastair Blanshard, *Hercules: A Heroic Life* (London, 2005); Mary Beard, 'Le Mythe (grec) à Rome: Hercule aux bains', in S. Georgoudi and J-P. Vernant (eds), *Mythes au figuré* (Paris, 1996), pp. 81–104.

BUSIRIS: Phiroze Vasunia, *The Gift of the Nile* (Berkeley and Los Angeles, 2001).

APOTHEOSIS: Mary Beard and John Henderson, 'The Emperor's New Body: Ascension from Rome', in Maria Wyke (ed.), *Parchments of Gender: Deciphering the Body in Antiquity* (Oxford, 1998), pp. 191–219.

LYCURGUS: Paul Cartledge, *The Spartans: An Epic History* (London, 2002); I. Malkin, *Myth and Territory in the Spartan Mediterranean* (Cambridge, 1994); A. Szegedy-Maszak, 'Legends of the Greek Lawgivers', *Greek, Roman, and Byzantine Studies*, 19 (1978): 199–209.

THESEUS: Henry J. Walker, *Theseus and Athens* (New York, 1994).

Chapter 4

MUTHOS AND *LOGOS*: Richard Buxton (ed.), *From Myth to Reason: Studies in the Development of Greek Thought* (Oxford, 1999).

HISTORY OF 'MYTHOLOGY': Fritz Graf, *Greek Mythology: An Introduction*, tr. T. Marier (Baltimore and London, 1993); Bruce Lincoln, *Theorizing Myth: Narrative, Ideology, and Scholarship* (Chicago and London, 1999).

PLATO ON MYTH: M. M. McCabe, 'Myth, Allegory and Argument in Plato', *Apeiron* supplement to vol. 25 (1992): 47–67; Kathryn

Morgan, *Myth and Philosophy from the Presocratics to Plato* (Cambridge, 2000).

ALLEGORY: H. David Brumble, *Classical Myths and Legends in the Middle Ages and Renaissance* (London, 1998).

OVID *METAMORPHOSES*: Elaine Fantham, *Ovid's Metamorphoses* (Oxford, 2004).

HERACLITUS: Jacob Stern, 'Heraclitus the Paradoxographer', *Transactions of the American Philological Association*, vol. 133.1 (Spring 2003): 51–97.

OVID MORALISÉ: Renate Blumenfeld-Kosinski, *Reading Myth: Classical Mythology and its Interpretations in Medieval French Literature* (Stanford, 1997), ch. 3; Raphael Lyne, *Ovid's Changing Worlds. English 'Metamorphoses' 1567–1632* (Oxford, 2001), esp. pp. 29–53.

Chapter 5

PSYCHOANALYSIS AND CLASSICAL MYTH: 'Psychoanalytic Writings on Classical Mythology and Religion: 1909–1960', review article by Justin Glenn in *The Classical World* 1976–7: 225–47; Robert Eisner, *The Road to Daulis. Psychoanalysis, Psychology, and Classical Mythology* (New York, 1987).

MEDUSA: M. Garber and N. Vickers (eds), *The Medusa Reader* (New York, 2003).

FREUD AND CLASSICAL MYTH: R. H. Armstrong, *A Compulsion for Antiquity: Freud and the Ancient World* (Cornell, 2005); Christine Downing, 'Sigmund Freud and the Greek Mythological Tradition', *Journal of the American Academy of Religion*, vol. 43 (1975): 3–14;

OEDIPUS: Lowell Edmunds, *Oedipus* (Oxford and New York, 2006); P. L. Rudnytsky, *Freud and Oedipus* (New York, 1987); Jan Bremmer, 'Oedipus and the Greek Oedipus Complex', in Jan Bremmer (ed.), *Interpretations of Greek Mythology* (London, 1987), pp. 41–59.

ANTIGONE: Miriam Leonard, 'Antigone, the Political and the Ethics of Psychoanalysis', *Proceedings of the Cambridge Philological Society*, 49 (2003): 130–54; Vanda Zajko and Miriam Leonard (eds), *Laughing With Medusa: Classical Myth and Feminist Thought* (Oxford, 2006), Part 1 on Myth and Psychoanalysis, and Part II on Antigone, politics, and psychoanalysis.

CUPID AND PSYCHE: Christiane Noireau, *Psyché* (Paris, 1998); J. J. Winkler, *Auctor and Actor: A Narratological Reading of Apuleius' 'Golden Ass'* (Berkeley, 1991).

JUNG: A. Samuels, *Jung and the Post-Jungians* (London, 1985).

FUNCTIONS OF PSYCHOANALYSIS: Peter Homans, *The Ability to Mourn: Disillusionment and the Social Origins of Psychoanalysis* (Chicago and London, 1989).

Chapter 6

GENDER AND CLASSICAL MYTH: L. Doherty, *Gender and the Interpretation of Classical Myth* (London, 2001);

RAPE IN MYTH: Diane Wolfthal, *Images of Rape* (Cambridge, 1999); Froma Zeitlin, 'Configurations of Rape in Greek Myths', in S. Tomaselli and R. Porter (eds), *Rape* (Oxford, 1986), pp. 122–51; Sandra Joshel, 'The Body Female and the Body Politic: Livy's Lucretia and Verginia', in Amy Richlin (ed.), *Pornography and Representation in Greece and Rome* (Oxford, 1992), pp. 112–30.

SABINE WOMEN: Mary Beard, 'The Erotics of Rape: Livy, Ovid and the Sabine Women', in Paivi Setala and Liisa Savunen (eds),

Female Networks and the Public Sphere in Roman Society, *Acta Instituti Romani Finlandiae* 22 (Rome, 1999), pp. 1–10; Carol Dougherty, 'Sowing the Seeds of Violence: Rape, Women, and the Land', in Maria Wyke (ed.), *Parchments of Gender: Deciphering the Body in Antiquity* (Oxford, 1998), pp. 267–84.

GANYMEDE: Craig A. Williams, *Roman Homosexuality* (New York, 1999); L. Barkan, *Transuming Passion: Ganymede and the Erotics of Humanism* (Stanford, 1991).

CHRISTINE DE PIZAN: *The Book of the City of Ladies*, tr. Earl Jeffrey Richards, introductory essay by Marina Warner (New York, 1982).

MAUD SULTER: Sue Malvern, 'The Muses and the Museum: Maud Sulter's Retelling of the Canon', in Maria Wyke and Michael Biddiss (eds), *The Uses and Abuses of Antiquity* (Bern, 1999), pp. 229–44.

DEMETER AND PERSEPHONE: Helene P. Foley (ed.), *The Homeric Hymn to Demeter* (text, translation, commentary, and interpretative essays) (Princeton, 1994).

WOMEN POETS: Alicia Ostriker, 'The Thieves of Language: Women Poets and Revisionist Mythmaking', in Elaine Showalter (ed.), *The New Feminist Criticism: Essays on Women, Literature and Theory* (London, 1981, reprinted 1986), pp. 314–38; Zajko and Leonard (eds), *Laughing with Medusa* (Oxford, 2006), Part V on Myth and Poetry.

IRIGARAY: Miriam Leonard, 'Irigaray's Cave: Feminist Theory and the Politics of French Classicism', *Ramus*, 28 (1999): 152–68.

Chapter 7

NEW AGE: David Tacey, *Jung and the New Age* (Sussex and Philadelphia, 2001); William Bloom (ed.), *Holistic Revolution: The Essential Reader* (London, 2000).

ASTROLOGY: Tamsyn Barton, *Ancient Astrology* (London, 1994).

'HERCULES': J. Seznec, *The Survival of the Pagan Gods: The Mythological Tradition and its Place in Renaissance Humanism and Art* (Princeton, 1953), esp. pp. 155–60; Yves Bonnefoy (ed.), *Roman and European Mythologies*, tr. under the direction of Wendy Doniger (Chicago and London, 1991, 1992), esp. pp. 209–10.

THE GREAT GODDESS: Rosemary Radford Ruether, *Goddesses and the Divine Feminine* (Berkeley, Los Angeles, and London, 2005); Camille Paglia, 'Erich Neumann: Theorist of the Great Mother', *Arion*, 13.3 (2006): 2–14; Carol P. Christ, 'Why Women Need the Goddess: Phenomenological, Psychological, and Political Reflections', in Carol P. Christ and Judith Plaskow (eds), *Womanspirit Rising: A Feminist Reader in Religion* (New York and San Francisco, 1979, revised in 1992), pp. 273–87; Clarissa Pinkola Estés, *Women Who Run with the Wolves: Myths and Stories of the Wild Woman Archetype* (New York, 1992).

DIANA: Jane Caputi, *Goddesses and Monsters: Women, Myth, Power, and Popular Culture* (Wisconsin, 2004).

GRAVES: Penny Murray, 'Reclaiming the Muse', in Zajko and Leonard (eds) (2006), pp. 327–54.

BETSY DAMON: Gloria Feman Orenstein, 'Recovering Her Story: Feminist Artists Reclaim the Great Goddess', in Norma Broude and Mary D. Garrard (eds), *The Power of Feminist Art: The American Movement of the 1970s, History and Impact* (New York, 1994).

Index

Index

Visit the
VERY SHORT
INTRODUCTIONS
Web site

www.oup.co.uk/vsi

- ➤ **Information** about all published titles

- ➤ News of **forthcoming books**

- ➤ **Extracts** from the books, including titles
  not yet published

- ➤ **Reviews** and views

- ➤ **Links** to other **web sites** and main
  OUP web page

- ➤ Information about **VSIs in translation**

- ➤ **Contact** the editors

- ➤ **Order** other **VSIs** on-line

Expand your collection of
VERY SHORT INTRODUCTIONS

CLASSICS
A Very Short Introduction
Mary Beard and John Henderson

This Very Short Introduction to Classics links a haunting temple on a lonely mountainside to the glory of ancient Greece and the grandeur of Rome, and to Classics within modern culture – from Jefferson and Byron to Asterix and Ben-Hur.

'The authors show us that Classics is a "modern" and sexy subject. They succeed brilliantly in this regard … nobody could fail to be informed and entertained – and the accent of the book is provocative and stimulating.'

John Godwin, *Times Literary Supplement*

'Statues and slavery, temples and tragedies, museum, marbles, and mythology – this provocative guide to the Classics demystifies its varied subject-matter while seducing the reader with the obvious enthusiasm and pleasure which mark its writing.'

Edith Hall

ANCIENT PHILOSOPHY
A Very Short Introduction
Julia Annas

The tradition of ancient philosophy is a long, rich and varied one, in which a constant note is that of discussion and argument. This book aims to introduce readers to some ancient debates and to get them to engage with the ancient developments of philosophical themes. Getting away from the presentation of ancient philosophy as a succession of Great Thinkers, the book aims to give readers a sense of the freshness and liveliness of ancient philosophy, and of its wide variety of themes and styles.

'Incisive, elegant, and full of the excitement of doing philosophy, Julia Annas's Short Introduction boldly steps outside of conventional chronological ways of organizing material about the Greeks and Romans to get right to the heart of the human problems that exercised them, problems ranging from the relation between reason and emotion to the objectivity of truth. I can't think of a better way to begin.'

Martha Nussbaum, University of Chicago

www.oup.co.uk/vsi/ancientphilosophy

ARCHAEOLOGY
A Very Short Introduction
Paul Bahn

This entertaining Very Short Introduction reflects the enduring popularity of archaeology – a subject which appeals as a pastime, career, and academic discipline, encompasses the whole globe, and surveys 2.5 million years. From deserts to jungles, from deep caves to mountain tops, from pebble tools to satellite photographs, from excavation to abstract theory, archaeology interacts with nearly every other discipline in its attempts to reconstruct the past.

'very lively indeed and remarkably perceptive … a quite brilliant and level-headed look at the curious world of archaeology'

Barry Cunliffe, University of Oxford

'It is often said that well-written books are rare in archaeology, but this is a model of good writing for a general audience. The book is full of jokes, but its serious message – that archaeology can be a rich and fascinating subject – it gets across with more panache than any other book I know.'

Simon Denison, editor of *British Archaeology*

www.oup.co.uk/vsi/archaeology

GALILEO
A Very Short Introduction
Stillman Drake

Galileo's scientific method was of overwhelming significance for the development of modern physics, and led to a final parting of the ways between science and philosophy.

In a startling reinterpretation of the evidence, Stillman Drake advances the hypothesis that Galileo's trial and condemnation by the Inquisition in 1633 was caused not by his defiance of the Church, but by the hostility of contemporary philosophers.

Galileo's own beautifully lucid arguments are used to show how his scientific method was utterly divorced from the Aristotelian approach to physics in that it was based on a search not for causes but for laws.

'stimulating and very convincing'

Theology

www.oup.co.uk/isbn/0-19-285456-9

ROMAN BRITAIN
A Very Short Introduction
Peter Salway

Britain was within the orbit of Graeco-Roman civilization for at least half a millenium, and for over 350 years part of the political union created by the Roman Empire that encompassed most of Europe and all the countries of the Mediterranean.

First published as part of the best-selling *Oxford Illustrated History of Britain*, Peter Salway's Very Short Introduction to Roman Britain weaves together the results of archaeological investigation and historical scholarship in a rounded and highly readable concise account. He charts the history of Britain from the first invasion under Julius Casear ro the final collapse of the Romano-British way of life in the 5th century AD.

www.oup.co.uk/isbn/0-19-285404-6